BEYOND THE BIG

Published by River Grove Books
Austin, TX
www.rivergrovebooks.com

Distributed by River Grove Books

Design and composition by EVR Advertising
Cover design by EVR Advertising

Publisher's Cataloging-in-Publication data is available.

Print ISBN: 978-1-63299-994-8

eBook ISBN: 978-1-63299-995-5

First Edition

BEYOND THE BIG

TINY MOMENTS OF LEADERSHIP

JEFF EISENBERG

RIVER GROVE
BOOKS

Contents

INTRODUCTION 1

THE BIG THREE 5

THE TINY MOMENTS 17

1. Leadership Is Action, Not a Title 19

2. Are Leaders Born or Made? 23

3. Be the First to Strive 27

4. Little Things Aren't Little 31

5. When Did You Find Your Voice? 35

6. Own Your Leadership Brand 39

7. Have Humility 43

8. It's Always Too Soon to Congratulate Yourself 47

9. Be Fearfully Confident 51

10. Be Bravely Transparent 55

11. Credibility Is Earned 59

12. Eat the Frog 65

13. Ideas Without Structure Are Just Daydreams 69

14. Be Clear About the Why 73

15. If It Ain't Broke, Break It 79

16. Create Urgency 83

17. The Worst Decision Is No Decision 87

18. Unmet Expectations Are the Source of Conflict 91

19. Be a Role Model of Character and Ethics 95

20. True Character Is Revealed in Adversity 99

21. Be Mindful of Your Power 103

22. Care + Confrontation = Carefrontation 107

23. The Keanu Quotient 111

24. Birds of a Feather Flock Together 115

25. Win Hearts to Win Minds 119

26. Be Vulnerable 123

27. Remember Names 127

28. Manage Things. Lead People. 131

29. Delegate or Bust 135

30. Be Transformational 139

31. Be Gray 143

32. Who's Got the Monkey? 147

33. Stay Balanced Between Being and Doing 151

34. Encourage and Teach Critical Thinking 155

35. Be a Lifelong Learner 159

36. Manage by Walking Around 163

37. Trust but Verify 167

38. Enforce Accountability 171

39. Personify the Heart of a Servant 175

40. Wear the Right Hat 179

41. The Purpose of Power Is to Give It Away 183

42. Celebrate Innovation 189

43. FAILing Forward 193

CONTENTS

44. Recognize and Celebrate 197

45. Praise in Public, Criticize in Private 201

46. Change Demands Compromise 205

47. Make Their Personal Vision Yours 209

48. Take Fun Seriously 213

49. Feedback Is a Gift 217

50. Expect Growth 221

51. Be Interested, Not Interesting 225

52. Deliver Plus One 229

53. Worst Idea Goes First 233

54. Encourage "Intrapreneurship" 237

55. You're on Stage. Always. 241

56. Take the Bullet 245

57. Sacrifice Raises the Level of Commitment 249

58. Welcome the Messenger of Conflict 253

59. No Data Without Story, No Story Without Data 259

60. Protect Your Informants 263

61. Never Waste a Crisis 267

62. Deliver Your Best 271

FINAL THOUGHT 275

ACKNOWLEDGMENTS 277

NOTES 279

ABOUT THE AUTHOR 289

Introduction

THERE'S A misconception that pinnacle moments make great leaders. A singular crowning achievement, one sweeping motion:

You are a great leader because you guided soldiers to victory in battle.

You are a great leader because you delivered a speech that motivated people to take action.

You are a great leader because you built a Fortune 500 company—or saved an influential company from bankruptcy.

But leaders aren't great because they did just one thing right. There may be a single significant outcome, but there are a hundred decisions a leader makes along the way to set the foundation for reaching that singular milestone. A single heroic act doesn't deliver leadership; it's more like a puzzle where you add one piece at a time to get to the big picture. Leadership is built from each of these individual pieces, the "Tiny Moments."

Great leaders know that the best way to achieve real and lasting organizational excellence is by "baking" positivity, performance, and culture into the DNA of an organization. This is done by recognizing the collaborative efforts and diverse strengths of individuals rather than enhancing a singular aspect of your business. Taking small actions across a diverse range of areas plants the seeds for becoming a great leader . . . and creating others. Conversely, neglecting these Tiny Moments undermines the creation and preservation of organizational excellence.

In other words, it's not about doing one thing 100 percent better; it's about doing one hundred things 1 percent better.

I've seen the right question at the right time turn a skeptic into an advocate, a spontaneous challenge transform detachment into curiosity, and a well-timed compliment inspire newfound confidence. The philosophy of "doing one hundred things 1 percent better" empowers us to create a personal strategy based on the knowledge that comprehensive progress stems from refining many elements through the efforts of many people. When we channel their efforts and focus on multiple areas of a business, we create an environment that promotes innovation and growth for everyone involved. This approach also allows us to support individual development in a personalized way.

By examining these seemingly minor leadership moments, we can unveil the profound impact they can have on shaping and achieving a company's vision, illustrating how every interaction and decision connects to organizational purpose.

In this book, I share a lifetime of small yet impactful lessons learned through a journey in both professional sports and business. As a senior sports marketing executive, I led business teams for the Philadelphia Phillies, the Milwaukee Brewers, and the Buffalo Sabres, among other top-tier franchises, building highly respected brands and consistently growing revenue to historical highs. As president and CEO of EVR Advertising, I transformed a small boutique agency into a regional powerhouse celebrated for strategic innovation and meaningful client relationships. In all of these positions, I maintained an unwavering commitment to the small, personal interactions that shape effective leadership and highly functioning teams.

In these pages, you'll find actionable insights, rooted in both wins and mistakes, that illustrate how small moments can foster positive change, inspire people, and create lasting organizational strength. The concepts I explore aren't revolutionary. Many are obvious enough almost to be cliché.

But clichés are at least to some degree fundamentally true, so what I hope to do is offer a new way of looking at these concepts. My goal is to whittle down broad, sweeping ideas to bite-sized pieces that are easy to consume, understand, and implement. We'll further explore these concepts by looking at real-life examples of how these ideas make a difference.

I hope to inspire you to embrace these tiny, intentional steps in your own leadership journey, helping you achieve excellence—one meaningful moment at a time.

MANAGEMENT ≠ LEADERSHIP

I agree with Seth Godin when he says the word "manager" and the word "leader" mean something quite different. Managers are supervisors tasked with keeping things organized and producing specific results. They take an established process and endeavor to make it efficient. Leaders, on the other hand, create a vision for making change. They influence, inspire, and create an environment that cultivates change. Leadership has an exponential and sustained multiplying effect. Of all the kinds of human capital, exceptional leadership may well be the most rare and precious.

You can gain the skills to be a manager, but you can't learn how to WANT to be an inspiring leader. It's either something you strive for, or you don't. Many managers have no interest in inspiring greatness in others. In their relentless drive to create more efficiency out of established processes, they don't care about the people behind the profits. They fail to realize that a leadership approach that prioritizes individual growth fosters a workplace in which people are motivated by innovation and empowered to reach their full potential, which invariably leads to greater organizational success.

Leaders are often seen as having a high-level, freehand view of the big picture, leaving the details to those in the lower ranks. However, the best leaders aren't afraid to get involved at every level or to pay attention to the details. Attention is one of the most undervalued and unappreciated attributes we can possess.

Great leaders have a knack for thinking big and understanding small.

They shift from the left brain to the right brain in the blink of an eye, reacting with both their minds and their hearts.

As American diplomat Harlan Cleveland described it: "Leaders are problem solvers by talent and temperament, and by choice."[1]

Many of us have experienced tension when people in management roles don't think or behave like good leaders. They may display non-leadership behaviors such as selfishness, lack of empathy, micromanagement, resistance to change, or failure to give others credit. But it doesn't have to be this way. By becoming someone who values self-awareness, continuous learning, and genuine concern for others, managers can cultivate an environment where individuals are inspired not only to grow personally but also to elevate those around them. In other words, managers can become leaders.

This book is for anyone who wants to lead, from those who have never done it before to those who are ready to inspire greatness in others. You don't need a title next to your name to have leadership presence and take action. Anyone can assume a leadership role.

If you picked up this book, you are likely looking for guidance and insight into what it means to be a good leader. This drive and curiosity are the first big step toward leadership greatness.

Let's take the next step.

The Big Three

BEFORE WE dive into the Tiny Moments of leadership, let's first talk about the Big Three Ideas or the maxims of leadership that underpin these moments: vision, character, and abundance. These principles aren't optional; they are essential and ever-present for effective leadership. While specific situations might demand a greater focus on one principle over the others, leaders must always keep this powerful trio at the forefront of their minds, ensuring each decision and action aligns with these overarching ideas.

Let's look at each of them.

VISION
Change, Urgency, Transformation, Failure

Everything starts with a vision. Working without this clear picture is like trying to find your way in the dark without a flashlight. A company vision encapsulates its long-term aspirations and purpose, providing a clear, inspiring picture of the organization's desired achievements and objectives. A well-crafted vision statement acts as a foundation for strategic decisions, influencing the company's culture and serving as a constant reminder of its ultimate goals in the dynamic business landscape.

A shared vision is a compass that aligns everyone in the right direction, amps up enthusiasm, and creates a team mindset. With a clear vision, individual tasks suddenly become more than jobs; they become part of a bigger mission. As famed author and speaker Simon Sinek says, "Vision is a destination—a fixed point to which we focus all effort."

Company vision begins with the aspiration and inspiration of its leaders. They shape the overarching purpose and goals, providing a guiding light that inspires change, unifies the entire team, and becomes transformational. However, this vision is not created in a bubble and then handed down like a tablet from Mount Sinai. A vision's successful realization relies on the committed buy-in, dedicated execution, and collective efforts of the leader and staff, who ultimately translate the vision into tangible actions through a sense of urgency.

Once the company vision is decided on, it must remain top-of-mind. It's not okay to write it down, bury it somewhere, and then never revisit it. The vision must become a celebrated theme. Furthermore, it must be something that people feel and cherish, not just read and recite. Only then can the vision be turned into action and realized.

This alignment of goals and effective communication becomes crucial for turning vision into reality.

My professional philosophy is to center company vision around building and retaining an exceptional team that is passionate and cohesive. I believe a company that prioritizes professional growth for its employees cultivates a lifelong learning environment that fosters skilled individuals who contribute significantly to overall prosperity. This ultimately becomes a workplace "brand" that attracts other top-tier talent.

By articulating a compelling vision, you give your brand a distinct personality and purpose, making it more than a mere commodity. This narrative becomes a guiding force, aligning your team's efforts and resonating with customers.

As your brand becomes synonymous with a particular set of values and goals, it establishes a lasting connection with both employees and customers, building trust and loyalty that transcends individual transactions. In essence, a robust vision is the cornerstone of a brand's identity, shaping its trajectory in the market and influencing its sustainability.

Creating a company's vision is the perfect introduction to a book dedicated to Tiny Moments. It sets the stage for understanding how leadership, even in seemingly insignificant moments, plays a crucial role in realizing that vision. Tiny leadership moments, though often overlooked, are the building blocks that contribute to the larger narrative of a company's success.

Change, urgency, transformation, and failure are all factors in realizing the company's vision. These are concepts embodied in leadership and demonstrated to team members so that they eventually embrace them, too.

Change

In the dynamic interplay between leadership and staff, leaders must articulate a compelling and forward-thinking direction for the organization that provides the rationale for change. John P. Kotter, Harvard professor and founder of Kotter International, said, "Leaders establish the vision for the future and set the strategy for getting there; they cause change. They motivate and inspire others to go in the right direction, and they, along with everyone else, sacrifice to get there."

A culture of embracing positive change must start from the top because leadership plays a crucial role in shaping the values, attitudes, and behaviors of those around them. When leaders commit to positive change, they actively encourage and support it, setting the tone for the entire organization.

Urgency

Urgency becomes a driving force for adaptation and innovation in times of rapid change and uncertainty. Leaders who convey a sense of urgency effectively communicate the importance of seizing opportunities and addressing challenges promptly. This proactive approach not only enhances productivity but also instills a collective focus on achieving objectives guided by the company vision.

However, urgency isn't about doing things faster; it's about doing things better by focusing on what's important. Urgency motivates people to evaluate the status quo and challenges them to find new and better ways to get things done.

You can't achieve transformation without urgency.

Transformation

Great leaders expect more than just excellence; they look to transform people and organizations. Transformation, like change, is guided by company vision. Without knowing the direction and the destination, how will you know if the transformation is complete? Leaders set the tone by sharing power, asking the people around them for suggestions, delegating tasks, and cultivating a culture of transformational mentality where change is not only welcomed but also expected.

As Rear Admiral Grace Hopper said, "The most dangerous phrase [someone] can use is 'We've always done it that way.'"[1]

Companies that don't change stagnate.

Failure

Great leaders encourage the people around them to step up and take initiative. They give their teams the security of knowing that failures are not the end; they are opportunities to evolve and grow. As Henry Ford once said, "The only real mistake is the one from which we learn nothing."[2]

Thomas Edison said, "I have not failed. I've just found 10,000 ways that won't work."[3] Often, failures can lead to successful developments because only by seeing what doesn't work can you discover what does. Failure often prompts you to explore new approaches and think outside the box. When one method doesn't work, it forces you to be innovative and find alternative solutions. This can lead to breakthroughs, unique perspectives, and creative problem-solving.

Without a vision, the journey feels like a series of random steps, and the destination is a bit of a mystery. A well-spelled-out vision breathes life into your dreams, turning them into a story that propels everyone forward.

The result of a vision realized through change, urgency, transformation, and failure is a company culture in which everyone pulls in the same direction, promoting innovation and resilience and ultimately driving the organization toward sustained success.

CHARACTER
Trust, Integrity, Humility, Transparency

Since people in the workplace tend to reflect the behavior of their leaders, leaders must be exceptional role models. As the Chinese proverb says, "The fish rots from the head." If leaders are self-serving, arrogant, or abrasive, that style will trickle down throughout the entire organization.

Leaders are influencers in the workplace. Influence amplifies and heightens the perceptions of who we are, so character defects become more pronounced when people move into leadership roles. If you think of it like parenting, our leaders are the parents we rely on to teach us how to react and behave in times of tragedy and triumph. People rarely rise above the leader's morality and ethics.

In his acclaimed book *The Five Dysfunctions of a Team*, Patrick Lencioni uses a fable to outline what he sees as the leading indications that a team is in trouble. The first item on his list is the absence of trust.[4] Trust is the cornerstone and the foundation of all leadership. You can't lead without it.

The other four items on the list—fear of conflict, lack of commitment, avoidance of accountability, and inattention to results—all stem from trust issues. As leaders, recognizing and addressing these trust-related dysfunctions becomes paramount in fostering a healthy team environment and laying the groundwork for sustainable success.

As in life, there's a lot about business that is uncertain. We must take things with confidence and faith, or else we won't do anything. Inaction through overthinking is known as "paralysis by analysis." Sometimes, we must move forward, even though we don't know everything or can't be fully confident.

This is where trust comes in, along with the importance of leaders earning it.

Trust

Trust is the currency that builds strong relationships and fosters collaboration within a team. When team members trust their leader, they are more likely to be open, communicative, and willing to take risks. Trust engenders a positive work culture where individuals feel secure, valued, and motivated to contribute their best efforts.

Trust establishes credibility for the leader, empowering their ability to navigate challenges, inspire confidence, and garner support during times of change. When there's trust, the team is more likely to follow a leader's guidance with confidence. Ultimately, trust creates a foundation for loyalty, commitment, and sustained success within teams and organizations. According to motivational speaker Brian Tracy, "The glue that holds all relationships together—including the relationship between the leader and the led—is trust, and trust is based on integrity."[5]

Trust doesn't come automatically. You cannot simply demand it without earning it. You can only cultivate trust through a combination of integrity, humility, and transparency.

Proving you trust others is also critical to influential leaders. Trust is a two-way street. That might mean giving away some authority at times and trusting your team's expertise. Doing so doesn't mean you have given up leadership or power. It means you are leveraging the skills of your team to help you steer the ship.

In an article in the *Harvard Business Review*, Paul J. Zak described research in which he found that building a culture of trust is what makes a meaningful difference in employee engagement and job satisfaction.[6] Zak studied oxytocin, a hormone that reduces the fear of trusting strangers and increases empathy. He found that when there is high trust and leaders ask for help rather than make demands, it stimulates oxytocin production. Zak's research revealed that at companies where there was high trust, employees reported 74 percent less stress, 76 percent more engagement, 50 percent higher productivity, and 60 percent enjoyment of their jobs.

To accomplish this, you must have confidence in the team's expertise, gathering ideas like valuable treasures. We need to understand that collective intelligence is greater than any one person's intelligence and take advantage of the blend of vision and diverse voices to help us make decisions. Only then can we foster a culture where everyone is trusted, valued, and integral to success.

Integrity

Integrity, as a cornerstone of character, ensures that leaders consistently adhere to ethical principles and demonstrate honesty to build a foundation of credibility. It's like the GPS for your moral compass, guiding you to do the right thing, even when nobody's watching. Think of it as the glue that holds trust together—and once it's gone, it's tough to patch up.

Integrity is about consistency between words and actions; in other words, you not only talk the talk, but you also walk the walk. When leaders embody integrity, they naturally cultivate a culture of integrity within their teams. It's not just about following the rules; it's about staying true to your values.

In essence, integrity serves as a moral compass, guiding leaders to make decisions that align with their organizations' values and missions. Demonstrating integrity not only leads to long-term success but also fosters trust and respect among colleagues and stakeholders. Ultimately, integrity creates a positive impact that extends far beyond the immediate situation, shaping the overall culture and success of an organization.

In a world full of shortcuts, integrity is your North Star, guiding you to stay on the right track with honesty and principle.

Humility

Humility is the unsung hero of character. It highlights a leader's willingness to listen, learn, and acknowledge their fallibility. It's not about being a doormat but rather about recognizing that nobody's got all the answers.

Mess up? Own it, fix it, and learn from it. Humility is the backbone of authenticity, the secret sauce that flavors your reputation. When leaders openly admit mistakes and show vulnerability, they foster a relatable and authentic connection with their team.

Humility isn't about playing small; it's about acknowledging others and being open to new ideas. So, in a world of big egos and loud voices, humility is like a quiet strength that makes you a better team player and leader.

My personal goal is to be a leader who's a force for initiative but also a maestro of collaboration. I don't want just to dream big; I want to gather the team's dreams and help turn them into realities. Then, it becomes a symphony of leadership where every note matters, and self-importance has no place.

Transparency

Transparency reinforces character by promoting openness in communication. It enables a leader to be candid about decisions, challenges, and organizational directions. When leaders share information openly and authentically, they demonstrate respect for their team's intelligence and contribute to a culture of openness.

Transparency is a big part of character and trust because it's hard to put faith in someone who keeps you in the dark. That doesn't mean you have to be open about every challenge, grievance, or disappointment that comes up; it means creating a sense of transparency in the "why" and the "how" of what you're doing. It shows that changes in processes or expectations don't come out of nowhere. It creates a sense of security in those around you, making them confident that the decisions have their well-being and concerns in mind.

The sum of these positive leadership traits—trust, integrity, humility, transparency—defines a leader's character and establishes a bedrock foundation of trust, ultimately leading to effective and lasting leadership.

ABUNDANCE
Presence, Inspiration, Motivation, Passion

It's not enough to have great ideas; leaders must inspire others to join their mission and to do so gladly and passionately. To start, you must personally feel inspired. It's nearly impossible to get others to follow you when you're not enthusiastic or excited about what you're doing and what you're asking them to do.

Abundant leadership is an approach that emphasizes the sharing of generosity and optimism through a mindset of availability rather than scarcity. The concept is not new: As far back as the sixth century BC, Chinese philosopher Lao Tzu said, "Abundance is a building block of sustainable leadership."

Willingness and desire to share knowledge and create an inspiring work environment are characteristics of abundant leaders. They enable a culture where people feel connected and genuinely involved. Abundant leaders understand that the more they interact with others, the richer the entire team becomes. It is about promoting a continuous flow of interaction that propels the team forward.

Your passion inspires motivation, confidence, courage, and gratification. It stimulates and uplifts. It radiates energy that others see and respond to. It is contagious. People gravitate toward personal inspiration and are motivated by it.

You don't have to be an outgoing extrovert to be an abundant leader. I know many great leaders who are relatively quiet and introverted. You can have a softened demeanor but still have an abundant presence.

Presence

You can't lead behind a closed door. You must be present and abundant with your curiosity, enthusiasm, and connectivity. Being present is the heartbeat of abundant leadership.

Being present is more than just physically showing up; it's about active engagement and genuine connection. This presence fosters a culture of accessibility, making everyone feel connected and valued.

Yes, an "open door" policy is essential, but it doesn't stop there. Authentic leadership involves reaching out with genuineness, curiosity, and enthusiasm, not putting the responsibility on your team to overcome busy schedules and vulnerability to initiate contact.

Presence is not optional. You can't be antisocial or closed off. People must be comfortable with you, and you must encourage conversation. You must invest yourself fully, obviously, and joyfully. Walk around and feel the team's pulse. Proactively connect with people. Initiate conversation. Ask questions. Listen. Share ideas. Give out compliments and credit. Celebrate victories with a high-five and maybe a funky dance move or two.

Basically, be the leader everyone wants to chat with at the water cooler—the one who's not just the boss but also the chief morale officer. In the words of baseball great Reggie Jackson, be "the straw that stirs the drink." People truly feed off abundant leadership, and they wither without it.

By being present, leaders demonstrate their commitment, build trust, and create an environment where every voice is heard. It's what transforms a workplace into a thriving community, where leadership isn't a title but a shared experience.

Inspiration and Motivation

Inspiration is the engine of abundant leadership. It's the art of igniting passion and purpose in others, painting a compelling vision that transcends individual goals. Abundant leaders are like inspirational architects, constructing a narrative that energizes and uplifts the entire team. Through infectious enthusiasm, they create a ripple effect of positivity, instilling confidence and belief in shared success.

Inspirational leaders don't just dictate; they catalyze, turning challenges into opportunities and fostering a can-do spirit. Their ability to spark a collective ambition transforms the workplace into a haven of motivation, where each team member becomes a torchbearer of abundant vision. As John Quincy Adams said, "If your actions inspire others to dream more, learn more, do more and become more, you are a leader."[7]

However, inspiration alone doesn't complete the job of leadership. Motivation, which incites action or behavior, is the complement to inspiration. Motivation is the drive or incentive that propels individuals to accomplish specific goals or tasks.

Motivational messages focus on encouraging immediate action, often through rewards, recognition, or goal-oriented strategies. So, if inspiration triggers the "Aha!" moment, then motivation provides the kick in the pants that says, "Let's get this done!"

In essence, while inspiration sparks a deep-seated feeling or realization, motivation prompts tangible action or change. Leaders frequently blend both approaches to create a holistic and impactful influence on individuals or teams. It's a mix of "feeling" and "get up and go" that makes a leader not just a visionary but also the ultimate cheerleader who rallies the team to conquer mountains.

Passion

If inspiration is the engine, passion is the fuel for abundant leadership. It is the force behind why we do what we do. When we love what we do, passion is what propels us out of bed in the morning. Passion makes us fully committed to our tasks and ignites a curiosity to learn and do more.

Passion is what transforms work into a labor of love and significantly contributes to success, even more so than talent and intelligence. "You don't follow your passion; your passion follows you."[8] As Simon Sinek wisely advises, "Passion is an output, not an input. It is the result of doing something we love."[9]

When we discover and follow a vision we believe in and find success in its pursuit, we experience passion. Success fuels passion more than passion fuels success.

In her book *Leading So People Will Follow*, Erika Andersen outlines five behaviors that indicate a leader possesses genuine passion:

- "**Commit honestly.** They genuinely believe in what they espouse. . . .

- **Make a clear case without being dogmatic.** They convey the power of their beliefs without dismissing or belittling others' points of view.

- **Invite real dialogue about their passion.** Their passion is balanced with openness: they want to hear and integrate others' points of view.

- **Act in support of their passion.** . . . Their day-to-day behaviors support their beliefs.

- **Stay committed despite adversity and setbacks.** Their commitment isn't flimsy. When difficulties arise, they hold to their principles and find a way to move forward."[10]

Leadership thrives when presence, inspiration, motivation, and passion combine into a magnetic force field of positivity. These attributes galvanize leaders and their teams, making work meaningful and inspiring action.

Abundance puts the magnetic force into action and transforms that action into shared success. As a leader, you're not just steering the ship; you're charting and inspiring a journey in which everyone plays a vital, harmonious role. And along the way, the Tiny Moments are what get you to your destination.

The Tiny Moments

I N THE dynamic realm of leadership, where grand strategies and monumental decisions frequently steal the spotlight, it's easy to overlook the small moments that quietly shape our journey. Yet, as we dive into the many facets of inspired and transformational leadership, we discover that big events are possible only because of the smaller actions that great leaders take every day.

Tiny Moments happen when a leader takes a genuine interest in an employee's well-being, listens intently to their concerns, or offers a word of encouragement.

We marvel at the charismatic figures who lead others to greatness. We analyze the strategies of visionary leaders who redefine industries and nations. We celebrate the moments of courage when leaders make pivotal decisions that change the course of history.

But what about the moments in between? What about the seemingly ordinary interactions that happen every day in the workplace or within a team meeting? These moments, often unnoticed and undervalued, are the ones I've come to call "Tiny Moments."

Tiny Moments happen when a leader takes a genuine interest in an employee's well-being, listens intently to their concerns, or offers a word of encouragement. They're the moments when a leader extends a helping hand, expresses gratitude for effort, or admits to a mistake. These moments are the lifeblood of leadership, the energy that keeps people growing and an organization alive and thriving.

Throughout this book, we'll explore the power and significance these Tiny Moments have in the realm of leadership. At the heart of it all is a simple truth: Leadership is not just about authority, titles, or grand gestures. It's about the everyday connections—the human touch and the genuine care that leaders demonstrate in all their interactions. It's about understanding that leadership is not a solitary endeavor but a collaborative and deeply human one.

As we progress through this book, we will explore practical strategies and insights to help you recognize, embrace, and leverage these Tiny Moments in your leadership journey. Whether you're a CEO of a multinational corporation, a team leader in a small startup, or simply someone aspiring to make a positive impact on those around you, the principles we'll uncover can apply to you. In the pages that follow, you'll become equipped with the tools and knowledge to incorporate Tiny Moments into your leadership style.

So, let's discover the hidden power of Tiny Moments, the moments that define inspired and transformational leadership. In the end, you'll find that most often, it's the smallest actions that lead to the most meaningful change.

I said at the start of this section that vision, character, and abundance create the three pillars on which leadership is built. Now, we're ready to turn our attention to the Tiny Moments that are the bricks within those pillars.

If you have big ideas about becoming a great leader, you must start by thinking small. Welcome to the world of "The Tiny Moments of Leadership."

CHAPTER ONE

Leadership Is Action, Not a Title

R EMEMBER GROUP projects in college? How often did you find yourself in a group that went off the rails from the start? One person did everything, or nobody did anything. The only result was aggravation.

While you can learn leadership theory in books or online, true application is learned through practice.

Someone may have nominated a "leader," but effective leadership was conspicuously absent. Or, in the absence of a designated leader, everyone waited and hoped someone would step up and steer the ship.

You may have been the one who stepped in if that's your style. Or perhaps not. In college, the result may have been a low grade; in business, the objective will be abandoned unless a leader emerges. The penalty for not producing results could be a demotion or the loss of a client. In a situation like this, you don't need to wait to be promoted or asked to lead. You can become a leader immediately by approaching it with a leadership mindset.

Most people don't want to lead; they want to be led. Researchers asked the question "Why don't more people step up when they have the chance?" They discussed their findings in a 2020 *Harvard Business Review* article, citing three perceived risks that prevent people from taking the lead:

- "Acts of leadership might hurt their relationships with their colleagues.

- Engaging in leadership acts might make them look bad in the eyes of their peers.

- [Being] blamed for the collective failure, and that that could cost them a promotion or future leadership opportunities."[1]

In my experience, there are additional reasons: Some people lack confidence and may not feel equipped with the necessary skills or experience to be a leader. Some prefer to work independently rather than being responsible for a team. Others have personal priorities that take precedence over their leadership aspirations.

We need leaders because countless people have an inherent need to be guided, nurtured, and supported. Leaders manifest as the natural order of things. If you step up to take on the responsibilities and practice acts of leadership, and if you're reasonably good at it, you won't need to declare you are the leader; people will see you as one. The chances are high that you will eventually get a leadership assignment and the title that goes with it.

However, you don't need a title to lead, and getting a title does not make you a good leader. If you hear about someone's promotion to management, you might assume they have excellent leadership abilities. But that is certainly not always the case. Tension results when people who are expected to be leaders do not think or act like one.

You must learn how to be a great leader. (You already started down that road by reading this book!) The first step is to begin acting like a leader. While you can learn leadership theory in books or online, true application is learned through practice. First, you must discover your leadership style, then craft your approach and personal leadership practices around that style.

The United States Chamber of Commerce has a detailed guide for finding your leadership style with handy links to leadership assessments. You can find it at: www.uschamber.com/co/grow/thrive/finding-your-leadership-style.

So, look for opportunities where there is a leadership void. What projects can you take on to demonstrate your leadership persona? Look for projects and situations that need leadership. Grab one, then another, then another. As you grow as a leader, you will gain respect as one.

A TINY MOMENT
Leaders Don't Wait to Be Led

Many years ago, I worked with an organization that had a weekly printed newsletter. When the woman who handled the newsletters quit abruptly, I turned to my team for suggestions on how to keep the newsletter going while I looked for someone new. There were four responses:

1. Wide-eyed stares and no ideas

2. Suggestions we postpone or reduce the newsletter

3. Brainstorm people for a temporary hire

4. And Jason

Jason was new to our team and new to the workforce. He had joined us fresh from college in an entry-level position. He followed me back to my office following the newsletter nightmare and said, "How about if I stay late and do the newsletters until you find someone?" This fresh-faced kid stepped up and offered to help with something he had no experience with and that wasn't part of his department.

Once I made sure he wouldn't have too much on his plate, I thanked him and said I'd follow up with him in a couple of hours to go over what he needed to do. By the time I got back to him, he was already on his way. He had reviewed a couple of previous newsletters to understand the layout and had contacted various team members to check the status of the content for which they were responsible. He consulted with the PR group that worked on it and just ran with it.

He didn't need me to show him anything; he only needed confirmation that he was already on the right track and hadn't overlooked something by being proactive. Proactivity is a fundamental Tiny Moment in leadership. Jason became a leader because he didn't need to be led.

It never occurred to him that it was the responsibility of someone more tenured or "higher up" to take on the challenge. He only saw a need and believed it was something he could do, so he raised his hand. He managed the next eight issues of that newsletter until we hired someone new. He wasn't just some newbie trying to prove his worth, either. It was in Jason's nature to take on everything he could. He wanted to understand the organization's full breadth, so he was constantly volunteering to help any team that might need it.

Jason stayed with me for several years, working all the way up to VP. When I left the company, I even suggested they let Jason take over my role as president. The "higher-ups" thought he was too young.

Their mistake.

CHAPTER TWO

Are Leaders Born or Made?

VINCE LOMBARDI once said, "Leaders aren't born, they are made." Perhaps I am not in a position to question the words of one of the greatest football coaches of all time, but I don't believe that's the whole story.

> *We need to stop thinking of leadership as a skill you're born with and instead think of it as a muscle you need to stretch and exercise.*

We've all been around people labeled "born leaders," but what does that mean? Are they innately visionary and trusting? Do they have empathy and humility in their DNA? Were they capable of inspiring people the day they were born?

The fact is you can learn leadership traits like any other skill. These traits might come more easily to some, but they are possible for all—as long as you want it.

The question of whether leaders are born or made is the wrong question. The only question that really matters is, "Do you want to be a leader?" If you don't, then all the skills you are born with don't matter. You're not going to use them. If you genuinely want to be a leader, there's no doubt that you can be.

A study at the University of Illinois suggests that leadership is 30 percent genetic and 70 percent learned through life experiences.[1] Yes, some people possess specific characteristics from an early age that align with leadership qualities—for example, confidence, empathy, and a natural ability to influence and inspire others. These traits can give individuals a head start when it comes to taking on leadership roles. However, the University of Illinois study supports the idea that leadership follows a specific, learned progression through external factors such as education, mentoring, personal development, and real-world experience.

The study identified a "three-legged stool" of being ready, willing, and able. People first become ready to learn about being a leader; they then become willing to learn the skills necessary to practice leadership; and finally, they're able to lead because they have the motivation to do it. The study goes on to say that until one achieves a certain level of readiness, one can't move on to the other legs of the stool.

Leadership is not a position you are born into; it's an honor you earn. It takes work, determination, and an understanding that it's in giving, not taking, that you gain the most. You will make mistakes; you will learn hard lessons. Your beliefs will be challenged.

We need to stop thinking of leadership as a skill you're born with and instead think of it as a muscle you need to stretch and exercise. Some people are born with the physical makeup that allows for easy muscle building, while others will need to work at it a lot harder. Either way, you need to work to build and maintain muscle mass constantly. Who becomes the next Arnold Schwarzenegger has less to do with what they were physically born with and much more to do with how they mentally approach life—and how they use their skills. Leadership is the same.

The debate between being born a leader or becoming one through time and effort is the timeless question of nature or nurture. While some individuals seemingly possess an innate flair for leadership, it is the confluence of experience, education, and relentless self-improvement that shapes the true essence of exceptional leadership. Just as a diamond requires cutting and polishing to shine brilliantly, so do those with potential require the refinement of learning and growth. The most effective leaders are not born leaders; they are made leaders through dedication, humility, and an unyielding commitment to becoming the best version of themselves.

True Leadership Is Felt, Not Seen

Gary is a friend of mine. He's a long-time leader in the energy industry, but you may not immediately recognize that when you first see him. When Gary walks into a room, he doesn't necessarily command the kind of attention we generally associate with a powerful and influential leader. He doesn't have a booming voice or an imposing demeanor. Still, if you have a conversation with him, you uncover the hidden charisma that lies within his deep knowledge and genuine compassion. It's in those moments that you realize he is the embodiment of leadership itself.

In this tiny but significant moment, it becomes evident that Gary's power is not in showmanship but in his authentic connection with the work he does and the people with whom he interacts.

People are drawn to him not because he demands it but because they sense the comforting and calming aura he radiates. It's the confidence of someone who has immersed themselves so deeply in their field that it becomes a part of their being. He may not wear the leader label like a badge of honor, but through his authenticity, it's clear that the impact he has transcends titles and formal recognition.

In the subtlety of Gary's demeanor lies a profound lesson in leadership. He doesn't need to proclaim himself as a leader because his actions and interactions with others do that for him. In him and the Tiny Moments he shares with others, we see that leadership isn't about self-promotion or seeking validation through titles and recognition. It's about making a difference, creating impact, and influencing others through one's dedication, expertise, and, most importantly, genuine care for the people around them.

Gary's example serves as a reminder that great leadership often goes unnoticed, like the quiet hum of a well-tuned machine that keeps everything running smoothly. It's not about shouting from the rooftops; it's about quietly, consistently, and authentically making the world a better place through one's actions. It's about allowing the work to speak for itself and letting your character shine through in every interaction. In the end, as Gary's example shows, the best leaders are those who lead not for recognition but for the sake of making a positive and lasting impact.

CHAPTER THREE

Be the First to Strive

EVERYONE LIKES to be the absolute best at something. They want to win every time, hear the accolades and achieve top honors. But sometimes, this can hold you back because you perceive not being perfect or great or all that good (but

Thinking we must be perfect prevents us from taking the leap that has the potential to reveal our greatness.

trying) as a weakness. You're scared to do anything because you're not confident that you're the one who should do it. You may freeze with fear: After all, there might be someone better than you at whatever you're doing, so why even try?

However, no matter how daunting, you must try. Franklin Roosevelt said, "Courage is not the absence of fear, but rather the assessment that something else is more important than fear." By pushing through doubt and fear, you already have more courage than most people, and they will take note of you.

Don't let perfect be the enemy of good. Thinking we must be perfect prevents us from taking the leap that has the potential to reveal our greatness. Don't be afraid to act before you're ready because you will never be fully ready to do something you've never done before. You can imagine what you might be like as a leader, but only when you do it will you know what kind of leader you really are.

In the words of entrepreneur Neil Patel, "I'd rather ride a real horse than wait for an imagined unicorn."[1] Instead of waiting for the impossible "perfect" that keeps you stuck and going nowhere, act from wherever you are. The current you—the one wanting and trying and learning—is more than enough to be an influential leader.

Nobody gives leadership to a select few; it is EARNED by doing what others shy away from. True leaders are not those who strive to be first but those who are first to strive. They are first to see the need, envision the plan, and empower the team to act. They give their all for the success of their teams.

You inspire others by being inspired yourself. Enthusiasm and openness allow those who follow you to feel the same things. Those you lead will also follow you into the dark if that's where you're going. They will mirror your anxiety, fear, frustration, anger, disappointment, and doubt. If you don't listen, they won't listen. If you don't learn, they won't learn.

As a leader, you must be the light that shines first, shines brightest, and shines forward.

A TINY MOMENT
Prove It to Yourself, Not to Others

When I bought my ad agency in 2011, digital media was just starting to go to the next level. At the time, we were doing websites and other simple things around digital content, but it was clear that it was gaining momentum. So I asked for a volunteer to take a deeper dive into it. Pete was a junior member of the team at the time, and he took an interest in the opportunity when no one else did. He took it on, not as a responsibility, but as a challenge. His competitive nature helped push him through the learning curve. He didn't take this on to prove something to someone else; he did it to prove something to himself.

Though the idea seems foreign to most people today, in the beginning, the digital landscape was a bit like the Wild West. So much was evolving and unknown, and there were setbacks and miscalculations along the way, but Pete stuck with it. He wasn't gunning for people to recognize him as some unbelievable digital "guru." He was striving to make sense of this new technology. He wanted to understand it because it was apparent that digital was going to become the new norm, and he knew taming the beast was essential to remaining relevant in an ever-evolving marketing climate.

A few years later, I elevated Pete to a VP position, above more senior people on his team. He didn't approach work like he was competing against everybody in the office, and he didn't let the decisions of his peers—regardless of their seniority—guide how he responded to opportunities. The Tiny Moment was Pete's decision to say "I'll do it" when the temperature in the room might have suggested staying quiet. Instead, he was the first one to grab it and go.

CHAPTER FOUR

Little Things Aren't Little

REMEMBER HOW I opened this book? "It's not about doing one thing 100 percent better; it's about doing one hundred things 1 percent better." This little statement describes the very core of how I view work and life overall.

Most companies are quick to point out mistakes and celebrate big wins, but few take the time to acknowledge quieter accomplishments along the way.

Think of how you feel when there's a significant event like a promotion, a marriage, or an extravagant gift. These occasions get a lot of attention because they're big, loud, and exciting. But when you think about it, you realize that these big moments are the culmination of a life of many less significant events. These little things are the glue that accumulates over time and leads to significant outcomes.

Small actions and habits practiced consistently can create substantial positive change in various aspects of life. They demonstrate attentiveness, care, and precision. In fields such as craftsmanship, art, or design, meticulous attention to detail is crucial for creating high-quality work. The seemingly trivial details can make a significant difference and contribute to a project's overall excellence.

It's the same in leadership. The Tiny Moments combine to create trust and dedication from those around you, which keeps your team going in a positive direction. If you're only looking to explore or create the big moments, you're losing a huge opportunity to make a lasting impact.

When we discuss the things that matter but are considered unimportant to others, we often overlook the simple to-do list. Most people make them, but they don't always give a lot of weight to all the things on that list, or they think that some of the "little" things on the list don't merit much attention. But they do. If it means enough to be on a list, by definition it is not a "little thing." It may be easy to check off (or ignore), but it's not insignificant if it means enough to write it down in the first place.

However, while many people make lists, only some make progress. You must have the discipline, insight, and fortitude to act and do the things on the list. The respect you give to things that others may label as "little" helps define how people view your leadership. These small moments of attention inspire others to follow your example. When they see you as a leader, even small things will matter to them if they matter to you.

Most companies are quick to point out mistakes and celebrate big wins, but few take the time to acknowledge quieter accomplishments along the way. Small gestures and acts of kindness can strengthen relationships and foster deeper connections with others. Taking the time to listen actively, show empathy, or express appreciation for someone's efforts can profoundly impact their well-being and the overall quality of the relationship.

Sometimes, the little things can brighten our day and uplift our spirits. A simple compliment, a thoughtful message, or a small act of kindness can positively impact the giver and the recipient. These seemingly insignificant moments can contribute to a more positive and harmonious environment. Something as simple as telling someone they handled a difficult client well or thanking someone for going above and beyond in a tight situation goes a long way toward creating a culture of gratitude. So, when you catch people doing something right, kind, or good, make a point to make it known.

A TINY MOMENT
It's in the Details

Back when I was a senior business leader of professional sports teams, I was a notorious list-maker. One might even call it an obsession. There was always a pen and folded sheet of paper in my pocket that would come out repeatedly as I moved through the building and my day. One of my good friends who ran the building would roll his eyes when I'd pull out my paper to make a note. He'd point out random, meaningless things, like a gum wrapper sitting ON the garbage can rather than IN the garbage can, and joke, "Be sure to put that on your list." But a few months after I left the team for a new opportunity, that same friend called to say, "Man, I miss your lists."

My lists help me remember all the small things that I would otherwise forget as I move through my very demanding days. I might not remember that someone left a towel where patrons could see it if I didn't write it down, because between noticing it and returning to my office, other important things would generally pull my attention in different directions.

Sure, I could hope that someone else might notice the towel, but my job as the leader was to exemplify that the small details are a big deal. My list wasn't about micromanaging; it was about ensuring that the Tiny Moments of opportunity weren't missed. As basketball coach John Wooden said, "It's the little details that are vital. Little things make big things happen."

CHAPTER FIVE

When Did You Find Your Voice?

I T MAY seem that some people are born with a clear and confident voice and identity, but the truth is that all of us must discover and test along the

As a leader, your voice is a powerful tool.

way before we fully realize who we are. Only when we work with others, test boundaries, and question possibilities do we understand what we bring to the table and how our gifts can benefit the greater good.

When we talk about voice, we're not talking about timbre or sound; we're talking about the way you act and communicate with others. A leader is defined by their voice. But first, one must find it.

To "find your voice" as a leader means discovering and embracing your unique leadership style, values, and vision. It involves developing a strong sense of self-awareness and authenticity in your leadership approach. It entails growing your confidence to know who you are and what you stand for. You have found your voice when you have mastered your personal brand and use it to influence people around you. You have learned how to project to the world that you can make a positive difference.

For leadership author Stephen Covey, finding your voice as a leader is so important that he added a sequel to his famous book, *The Seven Habits of Highly Effective People*. The essence of the sequel, *The 8th Habit: From Effectiveness to Greatness*, is encapsulated by Covey's appeal to leaders: "Find your voice and inspire others to find theirs."[1] Voice is Covey's code for "unique personal significance." He asserts that those who find their voice and help others find theirs are the leaders we need now and in the future.

In *The Leadership Challenge: How to Make Extraordinary Things Happen in Organizations*, coauthors Barry Posner and James Kouzes say that leaders must find their authentic voice to articulate their leadership philosophy to others. "Leading others begins with leading yourself, and you can't do that until you're able to answer that fundamental question about who you are," they write.[2] "When you have clarified your values and found your voice, you will also find the inner confidence necessary to take charge of your life."

When leaders find their voice, they understand what motivates them and what they are passionate about. They are true to themselves and their beliefs. They embrace their unique qualities, perspectives, and leadership style. Once they have all of this, they hone their communication skills to articulate their ideas clearly, express their expectations, actively listen to others, and provide constructive feedback.

Don't ever mimic the voice of someone else, even those you admire. Authenticity is essential for a compelling voice, and you can't possibly be authentic by imitating someone else. Lock into your voice, the one assembled by equal parts of your vision, values, message, and personality.

Finding your voice as a leader is a personal and ongoing process. It takes time and self-reflection to develop a unique leadership style that resonates with who you are as an individual.

Have you found your voice? If you're still piecing it together, or if you are always looking to refine it, consider these questions:

- Where are people struggling to coalesce around a plan to move forward?

- Where would my advice and influence fit in?

- What do people need from me?

- What's my personal brand?

- How do people respond to me?

- What do I do and say, and when is this most effective?

As a leader, your voice is a powerful tool. It shapes company culture, influences perceptions, and guides those around you in understanding the "why" of the work. So, discovering your voice—and recommitting yourself to follow it every day—can be one of the most critical steps you take toward being an exceptional leader.

A TINY MOMENT
Big Opportunities Aren't Always Obvious

My voice arrived when I was a junior in college. I was active in a campus fraternity but had never held a leadership role there except as chapter historian. However, that involved little more than keeping important fraternity documents and artifacts in order. Most of my fraternity involvement was social.

As the elections approached for fraternity president during my junior year, one of my fraternity brothers suggested I run for the position. I was startled by Ben's suggestion because it seemed obvious that Joe would take the role. Joe was the house manager and well-liked by everyone. Basically, he was Mr. Fraternity.

However, Ben's suggestion intrigued me, and I made room in my mind for the possibility I could win the election despite what seemed to be a more obvious choice.

So I ran, and although the race was tight, I won.

The year-long experience as fraternity president changed my life. That's what finding your voice will do. While serving as college fraternity president may seem trivial in the grand scheme of things, being a twenty-year-old in charge of sixty-five college students and a big house is a lot of responsibility.

I thrived in the position and learned more about people than I ever could have learned from any academic class. Most importantly, I discovered the sweeping impact of effective leadership and that I was pretty good at leading.

What I learned:

- People really need and want to be led.

- It's challenging to manage a diverse group of individuals.

- It's important to communicate, shoulder responsibility, and foster a sense of community.

- Acknowledging diverse perspectives and encouraging open communication are keys to building a cohesive organization.

I took those lessons with me after college, shaping a lifelong passion for leveraging leadership for positive good. It was all because one tiny conversation with a fraternity brother sparked a lifelong relationship and fascination with leadership, which set me on a positive path. I dared to dream, and as a result, I found my voice for a lifetime.

CHAPTER SIX

Own Your Leadership Brand

YOUR LEADERSHIP brand conveys your identity and distinctiveness as a leader. It expresses your values and speaks to your strengths that deliver value to others. It becomes your reputation, which like a brand, is a sense and symbol of who you are.

You want people to know what they are getting and how it aligns with their needs.

Being a good leader has become central to my self-image. Whatever I may be good at, my impact as a motivator and a shaper of lives around me is what I hold closest to my heart. I will be more effective if I understand that people will respond to me by how they view me, which is shaped by how I treat them. I take ownership of this perception by being mindful of how it is established and reinforced in everyday life.

I focus on not getting too high or low. People feed off a leader's actions and emotions; confidence and behavior are highly affected by the vibe they get from you. One of my mantras is, "Heavy is the head that wears the crown." It reminds me that with all the rewards that come with being at the top, there is also great responsibility.

What would you say if someone asked you to deliver an elevator speech describing who you are? Because our culture looks down upon ego, it can feel awkward to verbalize our strengths. You might not even know your personal brand—what you bring to the table that differentiates you from others. Nonetheless, it is vital to understand your brand and what it says about your leadership persona.

Start by completing this sentence: "I want to be known for being _____ so that I can deliver _____." When complete, ask yourself whether what you have written best represents who you are, communicates what you can do, and creates value in the eyes of those around you.

As the owner of a marketing agency, I'm often tasked with branding strategy for clients. Our team creates a distinct identity through messaging. Then, our client must support the brand through actions to reinforce it in the minds of those who interact with the company.

We often say, "The experience is the expression of the brand." A brand whose identity, strengths, and principles are clearly defined and remain consistent is a brand that's easy for people to connect with. You want people to know what they are getting and how it aligns with their needs.

Personal brands are no different than corporate brands in this sense. When people clearly understand who you are (and who you are not), it is easier for them to relax in your presence because you've removed a lot of the guesswork and tension that comes from trying to figure someone out for the first time.

Leadership and management journalist Sally Percy suggests taking the following steps to build your leadership brand:

- "Don't confuse your leadership brand with status.

- Base your brand on your passions.

- Know your [unique value proposition].

- Be unforgettable.

- Offer value on social media.

- Practice what you preach."[1]

Business author Tom Peters describes a personal brand as "your promise to the marketplace and the world." He adds, "Since everyone makes a promise to the world, one does not have a choice of having or not having a personal brand. Everyone has one."[2]

You are a brand. Define it and own it.

A TINY MOMENT

Decide Where to Plant Your Flag

When Kris joined my company as my ad agency's director of operations, she didn't consider herself a leader. Before joining us, she was an accountant in a back office, removed from the "action." As she grew in her position with me and took on more responsibilities, there was a light bulb moment when she realized that she had the potential to be her own kind of leader. She admitted that she wasn't sure what that might look like, but she was determined to figure it out. She started reading about different leadership approaches and enrolled in a yearlong leadership course.

As she worked through her studies, she discovered the quintessential Tiny Moment with big impact. She noticed that people would ask for a minute of their supervisor's time and the supervisor would often ask them to come back later or to wait until they were done with whatever they were doing. In a Tiny Moment of reflection, Kris decided she was going to do things differently.

Regardless of what she was doing and how much concentration it required, if someone came to her with a question, she temporarily put her work aside so she could address their concern. When I asked her about it, she said, "I don't care how busy I am; I want people to see me as the kind of leader they can come to and know I am available."

She added, "If I don't help them, their flow and productivity slow down. It's possible they can't move forward with their work until they get an answer. I don't want to put it off. This is my opportunity to define my brand as a leader."

Kris repeats this Tiny Moment daily. I've seen people knock on her door when she is deeply enmeshed in unraveling a complicated report. Even though it can't always be easy to have her train of thought disrupted, she stops and addresses their questions, and the person never feels like they are a nuisance or an unwelcome interruption. They know they can go to her for anything at any time.

Being a great leader isn't about doing everything outlined in this book every time, but it's about figuring out where you will plant your flag. Find the thing(s) that can readily define your brand and consistently act on them.

CHAPTER SEVEN

Have Humility

MANY ATTRIBUTES that mark great leaders and help them influence people around them are not unique to being a leader but are desirable traits for everyone. These traits transcend the work environment and can color everyday personal interactions. Humility is one such attribute.

As the old Italian proverb says, "Once the game is over, the king and the pawn go back in the same box."

Humility is an aspect of human behavior that is universally recognized and admired. I'm not talking about false modesty or the so-called humble brag, whereby a person wraps their pride in seemingly humble sentiment. I'm talking about genuine humility, an essential element of leadership magnetism.

The bottom line is that no one likes an egotist, much less a narcissist. People consider humble leaders more approachable, forgiving of mistakes, and willing to acknowledge others' work. They motivate employees to share ideas and work harder. Several research studies concluded that humble leaders listen more effectively, inspire great teamwork, and focus everyone (including themselves) on organizational goals better than leaders who don't score high on humility.

While humility might clash with our view of self-worth on its face, genuine humility isn't a lack of self-confidence or the presence of self-doubt. Self-esteem is a crucial concept when it comes to leadership and humility. Healthy self-esteem results when you're comfortable with who you are and don't need to prove anything to anyone.

This confidently relaxed vibe can create a very magnetic personality. I have long believed that people who lack humility suffer from low self-esteem. They're trying to build themselves up by painting a picture of self-created (and solo-created) success as a way of courting respect.

True leaders don't need to tout their successes, because their accomplishments speak for themselves. Leaders don't need to solicit respect when it's earned. Desperation drips off those who want what they haven't earned. It often comes off as unattractive bravado and empty arrogance.

Humility is an attitude of modesty that comes from understanding our place in the larger order of things. We may recognize our strengths, but we don't believe that sets us on a higher level than other people. It's all about not taking our desires, successes, or failings too seriously.

None other than Plato had this to say: "No human thing is of serious importance."[1] I believe what he means by this is that no matter what we do and no matter how big an empire we build, in the end, everything disappears. Everything is impermanent. That's a sobering thought. And one that should help us understand that we should never take ourselves too seriously. As the old Italian proverb says, "Once the game is over, the king and the pawn go back in the same box."

Part of being humble is the ability to accept criticism and use it to help guide improvement. It's always possible to turn criticism into something positive. You can mentor and lead your people more effectively by using criticism well. Be human and allow others to see this side of you as a leader. As former US Secretary of Defense Donald H. Rumsfeld said, "If you're not criticized, you may not be doing much."[2]

Remember that you can learn something from everyone you meet. Each person you encounter has unique experiences, perspectives, and knowledge that they can share with you. Even brief interactions with others can provide insights, teach you new things, or offer different ways of looking at the world.

Gratitude is the foundation of humility. It changes our perspective of the world by helping us acknowledge the goodness in our lives and recognize whom to thank for it. In short, nurture an attitude of gratitude, remain humble, and don't believe the hype. Noteworthy achievements are accomplished with personal skill and resolve, but also in partnership with other great people. Be proud of the road you've traveled, but don't forget to tip the driver.

You don't have to gush over others or divert credit for your success constantly, but it is essential to remain mindful that no success happens alone. Say thank you and acknowledge the work done by others that created your opportunity to shine. Make sure that the people who helped you are happy they did.

As one of my all-time favorite mantras goes, "Don't ever take yourself too seriously. There are billions of people in the world who couldn't care less." Now, there's some food for thought.

A TINY MOMENT
The Turtle Didn't Get There by Itself

I was in a brainstorming meeting with our creative director, John, and Diana, a new member of the team. As we discussed marketing tactics for a new client who was looking for something more publicly engaging than what they had done before, Diana was mostly quiet while John rattled off several ideas, running the gamut from whimsical to practical. He mentioned something that sparked additional development ideas from Diana, and they quickly found a rhythm that led to a cool idea that met the client's needs.

In a full staff meeting later in the week to review all the new projects in development, I asked John to share the latest project with the team. John, in turn, gave full credit to Diana and asked her to present it to the group. Even though he had come up with the original concept, it was Diana who brought a lot of the detail to the pitch that eventually sold the idea to the client. A lesser leader would have taken credit for coming up with the original idea, but John knew that it was important for Diana to feel empowered and recognized as a new part of the team, so he gave her full credit without pause. John didn't need acknowledgment as much as he wanted Diana to feel welcome. One tiny moment, one huge impact.

The reality is that rarely does one person accomplish everything on their own. As my brother used to say, "If you see a turtle on top of a fencepost, you know he didn't get there by himself."

CHAPTER EIGHT

It's Always Too Soon to Congratulate Yourself

I HAVE TWO egos: One side of me is tempted to take it a little easier when things are going well, while its counterpart refuses to be complacent. That side knows that complacency will hinder innovation, and I may miss critical evolving opportunities and challenges.

You must remain humble and remember that you are only as good as the next act in the play.

Resting on my laurels in my business life has always scared me. To guard against this, I must continually set the bar higher. When I reach a goal, no matter how great an accomplishment it might be, I will be content to remain at that level unless I set another, higher goal.

Many people do not see complacency as a pitfall. Instead, they interpret it as comfort, fueled by a feeling of well-being. Compare that with Merriam-Webster's definition of the word:

Complacency

1: self-satisfaction, especially when accompanied by unawareness of actual dangers or deficiencies.

2: an instance of usually unaware or uninformed self-satisfaction.[1]

By definition, there's danger in being complacent. That's what scares me. I'm like a business owl, always in 360-degree vision mode, looking around for something I want or need to know. I have spent my career in marketing and advertising, a very fast-moving business that is always in a state of change. Just think of how the world shifted in the early 2000s with the advent of social media and lightning-fast digital communications. Can you imagine taking on that business with a complacent attitude?

Complacency is a flaw. It prevents people and organizations from growing and achieving sustained success. It is fueled by feeling so secure in your work that you never level up, mistakenly believing the status quo will last forever.

That's when you lose your competitive edge, and your competition gains market share at your expense. It only gets worse when you lose your better performers and you're unable to attract new talent to replace them.

As Edwin Catmull, Pixar cofounder and author of *Creativity, Inc.*, said, "The need to challenge the status quo is just more obvious when you're failing than when you're succeeding. But it's no less urgent."[2]

Complacency is the enemy. For many years, I have lived by the maxim "It's always too soon to congratulate yourself." I know life has a way of throwing a curveball and changing the game just when you are ready to take the win and pat yourself on the back.

When print newspapers were where people got their news, I used to say, "Today's newspaper is tomorrow's birdcage liner." In other words, the good things you have done are wonderful and certainly contributed to your success, but what is more important is how you move forward. You must remain humble and remember that you are only as good as the next act in the play. The world is littered with people who let success go to their heads or who got comfortable or over-confident and stopped doing the things that got them there in the first place.

When you start believing your press releases, you are in trouble. Anything that detracts you from looking forward, seeing the next destination, and moving ahead is a danger to you and your business. It takes focus, drive, and energy to keep pushing like this. As the leader of a successful organization, you must be a beacon of innovation, ambition, and growth. There is simply no room for complacency in a thriving business world.

In the words of leadership expert Warren Bennis, "The manager accepts the status quo; the leader challenges it."[3]

A TINY MOMENT
You Get Nowhere by Standing Still

The media industry is rich with lessons about the importance of keeping confidence in check. My friend Joe, who headed up a region for a large digital radio service, went through an experience that illustrates this well. He now knows the danger of complacency all too well.

The day the company won two major accounts felt like a triumph. Excitement swelled within the team, and a sense of accomplishment filled the office. Joe reveled in the victory but knew better than to bask in the glory for too long. He recognized the potential danger of complacency creeping in after the recent wins.

The following day brought an unexpected blow—the loss of one of their biggest clients. The office atmosphere shifted from celebratory to tense, and a subtle undercurrent of anxiety coursed through the team.

Rather than succumbing to disappointment, Joe saw this as an opportunity to teach his staff a valuable lesson. He called a team meeting that turned out to be a Tiny Moment of learning for all. He openly acknowledged the setback and the impact it had on everyone. Joe emphasized the need for continuous improvement and an unending proactive approach to their work. He reminded his team that in the fast-paced and ever-evolving media industry, resting on one's laurels is not an option. "If you are not moving forward, you are falling behind," he said, driving home the point that it is never a good time to relax.

Joe understood that while celebrating victories is essential for morale, it is equally crucial to remain vigilant and prepared for challenges that lie ahead. He used the client loss as a catalyst for reflection and growth. He encouraged his team to analyze what went wrong and to learn from the experience. By turning the setback into a learning opportunity, Joe reinforced the idea that setbacks are not just obstacles but also chances to improve and innovate.

He also stressed the importance of maintaining momentum. Success requires not just achieving goals but also sustaining and building upon them. Joe's message was clear: To thrive in the media industry, one must be relentless in the pursuit of excellence. This approach not only helps in recovering from setbacks but also in preventing complacency from ever taking root.

Joe's proactive response to adversity helped to refocus and reenergize his team, turning a potentially demoralizing situation into a powerful lesson in resilience and continuous improvement. This experience reinforced the team's understanding that complacency is the enemy of progress and that success demands constant vigilance and effort.

CHAPTER NINE

Be Fearfully Confident

LEADERSHIP IS like walking on ever-shifting sand. It's not quicksand, mind you. It's not going to take you under without warning. But it can be challenging to keep your balance. Even when you are beaming with confidence, it's important to aim for a balanced position to avoid what some call the "entitled–fearful bell curve." In other words, be confident, but guard against over-confidence.

While strong ambition and the pursuit of success are healthy attributes that can spark innovation and growth, unchecked greed can have significant and detrimental consequences.

There are many cautionary tales to heed. Remember Blockbuster, the once-dominant video rental chain? As digital technology advanced and streaming services gained momentum, Blockbuster missed the opportunity to adapt and embrace these changes. The company held on to its antiquated technology and made critical pricing misjudgments. As late fees for rented videos piled up, customers began to feel frustrated and dissatisfied. Customer frustration with late fees and the emergence of more convenient and affordable alternatives caused Blockbuster to lose a significant portion of its customer base. The company filed for bankruptcy in 2010, marking the end of its era as a dominant player in the entertainment industry.

WeWork is another example of how unchecked greed and overambitious expansion can lead to failure. The company, which aimed to revolutionize the office space industry through flexible coworking arrangements, was initially hailed as a revolutionary success story, with a valuation that soared to astronomical heights. However, a series of decisions driven by excessive greed precipitated the company's downfall. WeWork's cofounder and former CEO, Adam Neumann, pursued an aggressive expansion strategy that involved rapidly leasing vast amounts of office space without demonstrating sustainable profitability. Ultimately, its initial public offering (IPO) filing revealed an unprofitable business model, excessive executive compensation, and a complex web of related-party transactions.

Both cases demonstrate that an unchecked pursuit of growth, driven by clouded ambition, can obscure underlying issues and lead to a disconnect between perception and reality. It highlights the importance of responsible leadership and decision-making to ensure a company's long-term viability and success.

In business, I always keep the "fearfully confident" mantra in mind and encourage others to do so as well. For example, this mindset is especially relevant when quoting new business projects. At my advertising agency, we do excellent work and are confident in our ability to perform and deliver. We often wonder if we should charge more when we quote work because we invest so much in people and infrastructure to be as good as we are and consistently produce positive outcomes.

It's critical to be confident while remaining a little bit fearful; that's what keeps you from going overboard. It's a very uncomfortable place, but that discomfort helps you make better decisions. There's a phrase I often use: "Pigs get fed, hogs get slaughtered." It's a reminder not to be greedy. While strong ambition and the pursuit of success are healthy attributes that can spark innovation and growth, unchecked greed can have significant and detrimental consequences.

The key lies in finding a balance between personal and collective well-being and recognizing when excess starts to create harm. A healthy level of apprehension keeps you grounded. You must lead confidently but maintain enough self-awareness that it doesn't tip into arrogance. Ask for feedback. Look for mentors. Command respect, but also give it. Consciously and repeatedly, make sure that your self-admiration is in check. Because if you don't, your path can quickly shift from upward momentum to a downward spiral.

A TINY MOMENT
Don't Underplay (or Overplay) Your Hand

When I was the vice president at the Milwaukee Brewers, we had a significant opportunity: upgrading three sections behind home plate to premium seating. The project was not just about making physical changes but also involved strategic pricing decisions that could have far-reaching implications for our revenue and fan relations.

We understood that setting the right price for these premium seats was crucial. If we priced them too high, we risked a backlash from our loyal fans and the possibility of these sections remaining unsold. The last thing we wanted was empty premium seats, which would be a glaring sign of failure and potentially damage our image as a successful franchise. Conversely, pricing the seats too low would mean missing out on maximizing the revenue opportunity that these upgraded sections represented. It was a delicate balance to strike.

Our goal was to find a pricing sweet spot that would allow us to sell out these premium sections, but not so quickly that we questioned whether we had undervalued them. If they sold out immediately, it would suggest that we priced the seats too low, indicating that we left money on the table. On the other hand, a prolonged struggle to sell them could mean the prices were too high, causing frustration among our ownership group and possibly leaving us with unsold inventory.

To navigate this, we embarked on thorough research, examining how other Major League Baseball teams had introduced similar premium seating. We looked at various factors, including market demand, fan demographics, and the health of the local economy. We analyzed both successful and unsuccessful case studies to understand what worked and what didn't. This research provided us with valuable insights and a range of potential pricing strategies.

Armed with this information, we held numerous discussions and debates, weighing the pros and cons of different pricing scenarios. We scrutinized each alternative to ensure we considered all possible outcomes. This deliberative process was characterized by what I like to call "fearful confidence"—a state of being cautiously optimistic yet aware of the risks involved. The Tiny Moment that unfolded during these conversations reinforced to the entire group that deliberate planning and strategic foresight can turn potential risks into significant achievements, reinforcing the importance of balancing confidence with caution in every professional challenge.

Our careful planning paid off. We set the prices at a level that struck the right balance. The premium seats sold out, but it took a couple of months of effective marketing and dedicated salesmanship to achieve this. This timeline was exactly what we hoped for; it was a clear indication that we had not underpriced the seats, as they didn't sell out immediately, but we also hadn't overpriced them, as they did eventually sell out.

The project's success demonstrated the value of combining research, discussion, and strategic confidence in decision-making. It also highlighted how essential it is to stay attuned to the market and our customers, adjusting strategies as needed to align with their expectations and our organizational goals. It was a lesson in how striking a balance between fear and confidence by being cautiously optimistic can lead to successful outcomes in complex, high-stakes scenarios. This approach, rooted in thorough preparation and thoughtful analysis, is one that I have carried forward in all my professional endeavors, recognizing that the right balance—in all situations—is the key to long-term success.

CHAPTER TEN

Be Bravely Transparent

WHEN YOU practice good character and ethical behavior, transparency follows. Transparency is one of the key components of honesty; it is open and truthful communication that provides

People are not looking for perfection; they respond to authenticity and honesty.

information, creates clarity, and builds trust. As former CEO of GE Jack Welch said, "Trust happens when leaders are transparent, candid, and keep their word."[1]

Workers recognize and appreciate transparency, and they value it. According to a study by the communication platform Slack, 80 percent of workers polled reported wanting more information on how leaders in their organization make decisions, and 87 percent said they will look for transparency in a future workplace.[2]

When you open the door to openness and candor, others will follow you through it. Workplace transparency fosters a sense of confidence, provides motivation, and unlocks the creative problem-solving abilities innate in everyone. Without it, there is a barrier between you and your people, preventing you from earning support and credibility, creating an obstacle to greatness. Even the Dalai Lama weighs in on this, often credited as having said, "A lack of transparency results in distrust and a deep sense of insecurity."

Being transparent can be challenging for many reasons, especially for people who guard their privacy. Others may postpone or avoid conversations about difficult or sensitive subjects rather than deal with the discomfort that sometimes goes along with transparency. While it's not always easy to tell the truth, overcoming that obstacle is necessary when you strive to be a great leader. Working through the discomfort often reveals the unexpected peace of mind that comes with being open and honest.

When a vision of transparency guides you, you are forced to work within a spirit of ethics. By being upfront and honest about your challenges, mistakes, and what you've learned from these experiences—even when it is hard to do so—you practice transparency. When in doubt, remember the words of John C. Maxwell, who said, "Speak the truth. Transparency breeds legitimacy."

Your example inspires others to follow your lead by building open communication channels with others at work. People are not looking for perfection; they respond to authenticity and honesty. As you practice transparency and have more heart-to-heart talks, you discover who can handle honest conversations and be transparent with you. Pushing for openness by exemplifying it may reveal those who struggle with being equally open, which could indicate they are not the right fit for your team.

A TINY MOMENT
When It's Dark, Add Light

At the start of the Covid-19 pandemic, like many business owners, I had to make a lot of big decisions on the fly. We were all in unknown territory and, as a leader, it can feel dangerous to appear vulnerable in front of staff. They will amplify whatever you express, so if you're unclear, they will live in confusion. As I looked around at how other owners were leading their companies through the early days of the pandemic, I saw a lot of confident proclamations that were obviously hiding uncertainty. Conversations were happening behind closed doors, leaving staff to wonder what was going to happen. I had a day or two of behaving in a similar fashion, but upon recognizing the bewilderment of my team, I pulled them all together to make two bold statements: "I have no road map for this situation and I can make no guarantees, but here is what I'm thinking," followed by, "How does this sound to you?"

My transparency allowed the team to feel seen and heard in their own confusion. There's a way to be confidently unsure that starts with the truth and doesn't feel like weakness. I told everyone that I had to make some immediate and difficult decisions to ensure we'd survive as a company while figuring out what the pandemic would mean in the long run. I had to lay off three people and reduce the salary for the remaining staff by 20 percent, all the while making a verbal commitment to do everything I could to make the team and the company whole again. I openly admitted that I wasn't sure if I would be successful or not. Because I had been transparent and laid the cards on the table, they trusted me when I said I would do what I could to figure it out for the sake of everyone.

It was a rough few months at the start of the pandemic, like it was for many companies, but we persevered because they knew we were in it together. In the end, we thankfully recovered quite well and I was able to repay all the missed salaries and hire back the one layoff who had not landed another job, all of which was wonderful. But perhaps the bigger story was the leadership that I was able to deliver in that one very important transparent conversation I had with my staff at a time of great uncertainty and angst.

CHAPTER ELEVEN

Credibility Is Earned

CREDIBILITY IS a must for great leadership. It is the foundation upon which you build trust, and without it, employees will lack confidence in what you do and will doubt your decisions. This erosion of trust can quickly lead to disrespect and even insubordination.

I realized that the team didn't need me to be a know-it-all; they needed me to listen, to learn, and to show that I respected their knowledge and expertise.

A leader builds credibility with a combination of credentials, competence, and character. Your experience and your education level, including degrees, certifications, and specialized training, initially establish it. But it doesn't stop there. Credentials just get you in the door. Ultimately, credibility is a blend of objective and subjective factors. Having experience and credentials alone doesn't guarantee that you will have credibility with those around you. How others view your credibility will also come from how you act and perform.

Firstly, you must show that you can turn credentials on paper into actual competence in the field. It's one thing to appear intelligent and qualified, but the real question is whether you can apply that knowledge when it counts. Can you translate theory into effective action with your team? It's more than just knowing the facts—it's about synthesizing information, building strategies, and performing under pressure. In short, how effectively do you execute your responsibilities in the day-to-day realities of your role?

With credentials and competence under your belt, you must now demonstrate the quality of your character to achieve true credibility. Your personal character traits are indispensable in completing the formula for lasting credibility. Those traits include being respectful, honest, competent, accountable, loyal, and trusting,

Credibility taps into the feelings and opinions others form about you. While your credentials and competence lay the groundwork for credibility, it's the intuitive gut feeling people get from working with you that solidifies it. This gut feeling is often shaped by how consistently you align your actions with your words and how dependable and trustworthy you are in the eyes of others.

Credibility isn't static; it evolves as people continue to interact with you and your character. For instance, an impressive resume might initially suggest credibility, but if you fail to lead with authority, neglect to follow through on promises, or act without integrity, that credibility quickly dissolves.

Without credibility, people will lose trust in you; and once broken, trust can be nearly impossible to rebuild. Therefore, maintaining credibility requires consistent character-driven actions that reinforce the trust others place in you.

Leadership scholars James Kouzes and Barry Posner address the characteristics of admired leaders in their best-selling classic, *The Leadership Challenge*. One of their key findings is that people identified honesty as more important than any other leadership characteristic.

"First and foremost, people want a leader who is honest, and they want to follow leaders who are credible," they write. "People must be able to believe in their leaders. To willingly follow them, people must believe that the leader's word can be trusted. If they don't believe in the messenger, they won't believe the message."[1]

According to their research,

"when people perceive their immediate manager to have high credibility, they are significantly more likely to be proud to tell others they're part of the organization

- Feel a strong sense of team spirit

- See their personal values as consistent with those of the organization

- Feel attached and committed to the organization

- Have a sense of ownership of the organization

When they perceive their manager to have low credibility, on the other hand, they are significantly more likely to

- Produce only if carefully watched

- Be motivated primarily by money

- Say good things about the organization publicly but criticize it privately

- Consider looking for another job if the organization experiences problems

- Feel unsupported and unappreciated"[2]

Credibility has taken on even more prominence in the age of social media, fake news, and the public's growing distrust of those in leadership positions whose behavior does not align with transparency, trustworthiness, and integrity. We expect more from our leaders than just being told what to do. We need to believe in them as people before we're willing to follow their lead.

Credibility is not something you claim or demand; it is something you earn and that those around you give you. Act accordingly.

A TINY MOMENT
Leave Room to Learn

After working as a senior leader in Major League Baseball and the National Hockey League, I transitioned to a new role as president of the Portland Pirates, an American Hockey League organization. I brought with me years of experience in sports leadership, but I quickly realized that my past successes and impressive resume wouldn't be enough to establish credibility in this new environment. I understood that demonstrating that I was willing to get my hands dirty and learn how to serve this team best, rather than resting on my laurels, would ultimately solidify my credibility.

Entering this role, I was very much an outsider in a close-knit community. Many of my staff members had worked with the organization for years, and they had deep roots in the area. They knew the ins and outs of the market, the fans, and the culture of the team far better than I did. While I had earned the job with my resume and experience, I knew that earning their respect would require more than just my past achievements. It would take time, effort, and, most importantly, a willingness to earn credibility on the ground.

From the beginning, I made a conscious decision to stand with my team rather than above them. I showed that I was committed to understanding their challenges and supporting them in whatever way I could. One pivotal moment that solidified this approach came in the lead-up to the first game of the season. The game night crew was preparing for their game presentation, and I met with them on the ice in the middle of the arena. As we talked about plans for the season, I shared insights from my experiences with the teams I had been part of before.

However, as I spoke, I could sense a disconnect and it was then that I experienced my Tiny Moment. While they recognized my experience, my words came across as assuming and perhaps even a bit arrogant. I realized that I had to change that.

The reality was that I needed a complete understanding of this marketplace before I could effectively lead. My past experiences, while valuable, were not a perfect fit for this new context. Recognizing this, I paused and took a step back. I realized that the team didn't need me to be a know-it-all; they needed me to listen, to learn, and to show that I respected their knowledge and expertise. So, I did just that—I listened. I asked questions, sought their input, and genuinely engaged with their ideas and concerns. In doing so, I began to earn their respect, and with that, my credibility started to take root.

This experience taught me the valuable lesson that arrogance and credibility are counterintuitive. Simply being a subject matter expert doesn't make you a leader; understanding how to read the room and apply your expertise does. Credibility is about more than just what you know; it's about how you use that knowledge, how you interact with others, and how you demonstrate that you are willing to learn and grow alongside your team.

As I continued in my role with the Portland Pirates, this approach helped me to build strong relationships with my staff, gain their trust, and ultimately lead the organization with the respect and credibility that are essential for any leader.

CHAPTER TWELVE

Eat the Frog

NO ONE likes getting bad news. This is why delivering it can be so challenging. You don't want to be responsible for creating the doubt, frustration, anger, or disappointment that bad news can bring.

Deliver bad news with integrity, kindness, and respect for others. Avoid assigning blame.

So, what do many people do? They avoid it for as long as possible. Perhaps they are afraid to cause disappointment or to be met with a negative reaction. This avoidance may be rooted in a genuine concern for preserving relationships and a positive atmosphere, even when faced with the reality of challenging situations.

However, delays invariably make the situation and the ultimate conversation worse. As avoidance continues, stress mounts. You think about how the conversation will go, what the response will be, and how the receiver of the bad news will respond in return. Frankly, you dread it. It hangs over your head and you might obsess over it. All the while, you are trying to go about your day, dealing with other issues and helping move the organization forward. It's all quite uncomfortable.

What does a great leader do—and teach others to do—when dealing with an uncomfortable situation? They eat the frog.

Mark Twain once advised, "If it's your job to eat a frog, it's best to do it first thing in the morning. And if it's your job to eat two frogs, it's best to eat the biggest one first."[1]

From that, productivity consultant Brian Tracy developed an "Eat the Frog" method that boils down to this: "If you have hard things to do, get them over with sooner rather than later."

Nothing good can come from the anxiety and "what-if" storytelling that can spiral out of control in your mind when you put off difficult tasks and discussions. It will only hang over you, dominating and affecting your day. It will detract from what you need to do. Take this advice and apply it to the tough conversations and unpleasant tasks that are inevitable.

Eat the frog. And do it as soon as possible so everyone can move on with their lives. As Forbes Council Member Charles Bankston says to his employees, "Run to me with bad news and walk with good news."[2]

Communicate bad news quickly. Not only will that unload the stress of what is coming and allow you to clear your mind, but it also allows you and everyone else to look for solutions and rectify whatever needs to be fixed or improved.

Let's say I have an account person who has just learned that we're losing a $50,000 job with a client because we screwed something up. That's certainly not news that they are excited to tell me. But I need to know the news because I'm always forecasting, and I might spend some money on something, thinking we have that $50,000 available. So, yes, it's true that I would rather not get this news, but I need the information as quickly as possible to do my job successfully.

The fear of delivering bad news could create an attempt to fix it or cover it up, which can only make things worse. I need to know if something's going on because I can't help address it if I don't know about it.

Deliver bad news with integrity, kindness, and respect for others. Avoid assigning blame. Be honest about the circumstances and take as much responsibility as makes sense.

Here's how (and how not) to deliver bad news:

- Don't sugarcoat it to the point that the impact of the news is lost, but do deliver it in a way that is easiest to receive.

- Don't walk into the room and blurt out the bad news without first reading what is already happening with the people you must tell.

- Get to the point quickly, but do so with a softball, not a grenade. This creates an opportunity for shared solution discovery and builds trust.

If I know I can depend on someone to share bad news with me, it's easier for me to leave them alone. I don't have to worry about them, and I don't have to ask so many questions. But if I know someone is more likely to hide bad news, I'm always worried and never fully trust them. If I ask them how things are going and they say, "Okay," I can only wonder if it really is okay.

A leader must value staying informed about challenges, both good and bad. However, it is imperative to establish a secure space for delivering unfavorable news. Leading by example extends to the leader's approach to sharing such news. Instead of reacting explosively, angrily, or harshly, the leader should exemplify a composed and understanding demeanor. This sets the tone for a culture of trust and open communication within the team.

Creating an environment free from fear facilitates the seamless flow of information, fostering effective problem-solving and continuous improvement. Therefore, the leader must not only expect transparency but also demonstrate it by promptly and tactfully communicating bad news, setting the standard for the team to follow suit.

A TINY MOMENT
Stand and Deliver (the Bad News)

Performance review time can be anxiety-inducing for any organization. There are conversations about metrics, bonuses, raises, and areas of improvement. It's awkward and can create an uncomfortable buzz around the office.

A few years ago, I had to have a difficult conversation with one of our team leaders at review time. Responsibilities needed shifting and the employee needed their responsibilities lessened to better align their current skill level with their workload. Kyle had been hired for a director position, which was a lateral move from his previous job. Unfortunately, the job with us came with elevated requirements that Kyle simply didn't have. I was not looking forward to the conversation, so I delayed it until later in the week.

However, the day before the planned review time, I pulled into the parking lot at the same time as Kyle. We walked in together and he asked my advice on a couple of the things on his plate that were challenging. I could feel myself being standoffish to maintain some separation before the crucial conversation I knew was coming later. I didn't like how it felt keeping him at arm's length for selfish reasons. The conversation was going to happen; that wasn't debatable. It was just that I, for whatever reason, wasn't ready for it quite yet.

I was uncomfortable with the situation, and it was preoccupying my mind, so I decided that I had to "pull the Band-Aid off" and get past this unpleasant conversation. When I got to my office, I immediately checked my schedule and called Kyle into my office that morning. It wasn't an easy or comfortable discussion, and Kyle was hurt and embarrassed by the demotion, but he said he could tell something was up when we walked in together earlier.

It would have been much crueler for me to let Kyle sit in wonder for days when he had a sense that difficult news was coming. As a leader, my discomfort should not be his to bear. In the words of former US Secretary of State Colin Powell, "Bad news isn't wine. It doesn't improve with age." Getting the truth out on the table sooner rather than later allowed for the healing and learning to begin.

CHAPTER THIRTEEN

Ideas Without Structure Are Just Daydreams

D O YOU know someone who is full of ideas but rarely follows through on them? Their ideas might be fantastic, but they're only collecting dust if there's no action plan. Often, it is only when these "thinkers" partner with a "doer" that anything of merit finally gets done.

Having a structure that results in the successful implementation of ideas requires accountability.

Great ideas are irrelevant if they only live in someone's head. You can't change the world (or even the paper in the copy machine) by just thinking about it. You need to formulate a plan and then make it happen.

Leaders must nurture ideas within a structure to be successful. This involves using systems and processes to provide the foundation for exploring, vetting, and pursuing these ideas. Structure is a set of malleable and agile processes that effectively keep projects and teams moving forward. Just make sure to distinguish structure from burdensome rules.

As a leader, it's essential to constantly analyze structure and systems to ensure they deliver as they should. This process ensures that those operating within the structure understand why these systems exist and how they work. Without this shared insight, people will skip or alter steps they deem unimportant because they don't see how each piece is crucial to the big picture. An uninspired manager says, "Do this," while a motivational leader says, "Here's what's important in this situation. How can we best go about our work here?"

Having a structure that results in the successful implementation of ideas requires accountability. Being accountable requires a personal commitment to a "see it, own it, solve it, do it" attitude. This environment can only exist if introduced and supported by leadership. Strong leaders allow the individuals on their team to own their portion of the process. In doing so, they are accountable for their piece of success.

When leaders micromanage and then claim responsibility for successes while pointing fingers at mistakes, they undermine their relationships with those around them and the project's integrity. The best way to avoid this is to establish a plan with all the proper checks and balances to ensure the best possible outcome.

Plan the work and work the plan.

A TINY MOMENT
Action Turns Dreams into Realities

Tobias was a young entry-level administrator at my ad agency. His journey into the world of graphic design began with a simple daydream. He had no formal training in graphic design, yet the creative work happening around him fascinated him. He found himself constantly pondering the idea of becoming a designer, but it remained only as a wistful aspiration tucked away in the corner of his mind.

As he passionately discussed his design ideas with friends and coworkers, a wise and perceptive one posed a short question that struck a chord, "Are you just gonna talk about it, or are you gonna do it?"

Fortunately, the same friend who had ignited his determination later offered more valuable guidance. Tobias was all ears. The friend reminded him that every expert in the field had started from the very point where he stood. The expectation of becoming a full-fledged graphic designer overnight was unrealistic and set the stage for potential failure. However, adopting the mindset of becoming a student of graphic design was a pragmatic and attainable starting point.

Embracing this wisdom, Tobias embarked on his journey with a resolve and willingness to learn. He eagerly explored the landscape of online learning opportunities for graphic design. But there was a key principle he held close to his heart—the word "beginner." It became woven into his mentality and he included it in every search and exploration he made into the craft, ensuring he wasn't overwhelmed or intimidated by advanced content.

His pursuit led him to a simple yet invaluable resource—a YouTube video on the basics of graphic design. This video not only outlined the fundamental concepts but also provided a structured path to start his learning journey. It included guidance on where to commence, what to learn, and how to transform his initial sketches—huddled in a notebook—into a digital portfolio.

Armed with this newfound knowledge, Tobias dove into the world of graphic design, one step at a time. He navigated the complexities of design software, patiently honing his skills and gradually building a repertoire of creative work. He was diligent, persistent, and unafraid to embrace the role of student.

A year later, Tobias had transitioned from his assistant desk at the agency into a role as a junior designer, all because he had experienced the Tiny Moment where he embraced the need to give structure to a dream. The structured approach he adopted to learning provided him with a clear path forward, turning an abstract desire into a concrete reality. It wasn't just about dreaming anymore; it was about doing, and in the process, he discovered the transformative power of structure in making ideas happen.

CHAPTER FOURTEEN

Be Clear About the Why

I DOUBT THAT anyone says they want to be a mediocre leader. Yet, when they aren't driven by a passion for why they do what they do, that is what they become. Without a clear purpose, even the most well-intentioned efforts can lead to mediocrity. Effort without purpose

We're not just creating advertisements; we're building relationships, crafting stories, and achieving remarkable outcomes.

is like rowing a boat with no destination. You may move, but you'll never truly arrive. Purpose gives direction, making every stroke count toward a meaningful goal.

A 2017 study by child psychologist Sam Wass, PhD, revealed that kids ask an average of seventy-three questions a day.[1] Children have an innate curiosity and really want to know how the world works. Asking "why?" is the only way they can learn. As they learn and grow, this curiosity can guide them to discover their passions and what truly drives them.

When was the last time you asked yourself, "Why?" When was the last time you paid attention to the choices you make and looked at the reasons behind why you made them? Adults don't ask as many questions as children, but they should ask even more.

"Regardless of WHAT we do in our lives, our WHY—our driving

purpose, cause or belief—never changes," says Simon Sinek in his book *Start with Why*.[2]

Imagine you're a curious four-year-old asking "why?" with each task you undertake. Consider peeling back the layers to reveal the true motivations behind your actions. Really consider what you're doing and the real reason you're doing it. That's when passion reveals itself.

Passion infuses purpose into routine acts, turning the commonplace into something significant. But the quest for this innate motivation requires reflection, a deliberate effort to uncover what truly matters to us.

When we engage in something deeply personal, something that aligns with our values and imparts a sense that we're contributing to a higher purpose, it becomes our passion, our why. And it becomes the driving force that elevates our performance and transforms our daily efforts into meaningful accomplishments.

Adults seek a sense of connection and a feeling of being part of something larger than themselves. According to leadership coach Jacinta Jimenez, "As human beings, we're wired to connect and part of purpose is serving others or serving the greater good, something outside of us that allows us to feel more connected. It's built into our DNA."[3]

You have a fantastic opportunity to reinforce your company's values, ignite your team's passion, and invite everyone to buy in by explaining the why behind the work. In turn, people see that you are driven by not only what is best for the company but also what is best and most motivating for the people in the company. They can see how they're serving the greater good through individual actions.

A world without a why can feel directionless and lack a sense of meaning. Individuals may find themselves going through the motions without a clear connection to the motivations behind their actions. As a result, the routine of daily life may become monotonous, and accomplishments may feel hollow or insignificant. The human spirit thrives on purpose, and the absence of a guiding force can leave individuals adrift and searching for significance.

Leaders overlook the why when they prioritize the "what" and "how" as the fastest way to influence their audience. They may think the answer to why is self-evident and doesn't need clarification. However, as professionals, understanding the why behind our work is crucial. When individuals align themselves with their underlying motivations, it becomes more than just a workplace; it becomes a community with a collective purpose. The why then evolves from a lofty mission statement into an integral part of everyday work life, motivating individuals to contribute meaningfully and fostering a sense of fulfillment.

As an example, Apple's "why" goes beyond merely selling products. It delves into a broader aspiration of enhancing the lives of individuals—students, educators, creative professionals, and consumers—through innovation. The focus is on creating an experience rather than just a product, reflecting a deeper sense of purpose and a dedication to making a positive impact on people's lives. Apple's why is about empowering and enriching the lives of individuals through technology.

This act of making a positive impact on people's lives is a powerful motivator. When individuals connect their work to a lofty aspiration, they become highly motivated to deliver their best work, driven not solely by corporate success but by a profound commitment to enriching the lives of others.

So, what is your organization's "Why"?

A TINY MOMENT
Big Clarity from a Small Discussion

Like any job, working at an advertising agency has its highs and lows. The fast-paced, consuming work is fulfilling and rewarding for those who are well-suited for this type of environment. But even those of us who are a good fit have days that are a little rough.

It is for times like these that we set out to understand our passion for the business or, put another way, our why. We planned to explore this at an upcoming retreat, setting aside a session to discuss this as a group. This session became a Tiny Moment that offered tremendous clarity for all of us.

After a discussion, we landed on three aspects of our job we were passionate about: people, creativity, and success.

First and foremost, people are at the heart of everything we do. Whether it's the clients we work with or our colleagues in the agency, building relationships and collaboratively working together is what drives us. The bonds we form with our clients are based on trust and a shared vision for their brand's success. Within our team, the camaraderie and mutual support create an environment where ideas can flow freely and everyone feels valued. Knowing that our work has a positive impact on others and helps businesses thrive is incredibly motivating. It's the people who bring energy, inspiration, and meaning to our daily work.

Creativity is the lifeblood of our agency. The thrill of coming up with a novel idea, the process of bringing that idea to life, and the satisfaction of seeing it resonate with an audience are unmatched. Our brainstorming sessions are dynamic, often producing unexpected and exciting results. The creative challenges we face push us to be innovative and constantly evolve. Every project is a new opportunity to explore different perspectives, experiment with innovative solutions, and express our artistic talents. This creativity isn't just about producing ads—it's about problem-solving, storytelling, and making a lasting impact through our work.

Success, in its many forms, is another key motivator for us. There's a profound sense of accomplishment in seeing our campaigns achieve their objectives, whether it's enhancing a client's brand awareness, boosting sales, or winning industry awards. Success validates our hard work and reaffirms our expertise. It also provides us with tangible goals to strive for and milestones to celebrate. Each success story is a testament to our agency's dedication, skill, and perseverance. It fuels our ambition to keep pushing boundaries and achieving greater heights.

These three elements—people, creativity, and success—are deeply intertwined and collectively define our purpose. They remind us why we chose this profession and why we continue to pour our hearts into it every day. Understanding our why gives us strength on challenging days and adds a deeper dimension to our work. It's a reminder that we're not just creating advertisements; we're building relationships, crafting stories, and achieving remarkable outcomes.

As we wrapped up the session, a sense of renewed energy and clarity was evident in the team. We left the retreat with a stronger connection to our mission and each other. Knowing our why has become a guiding light, helping us navigate the highs and lows of the advertising world with passion and purpose. This Tiny Moment of discovery has had a lasting impact, reinforcing our commitment to excellence and our love for what we do.

CHAPTER FIFTEEN

If It Ain't Broke, Break It

MOST PEOPLE dislike change. Change can disrupt familiar routines, introduce uncertainty, and require individuals to adapt to new circumstances. They avoid, tolerate, or are dragged into it kicking and screaming. As a result, change can often make individuals experience various emotional reactions, such as fear, skepticism, or a sense of loss. These reactions can lead to resistance to change. Therefore, advocating for change in what seems to be a perfectly adequate situation can be met with apprehension or straight-out rebellion.

If we do not embrace change, we can easily and quickly settle into a rut that can devolve into uninspired inertia.

"Everything is fine. Leave it be." Or, as the old saying goes, "If it ain't broke, don't fix it."

To me, "fine" means just okay, which is simply not good enough. Remember when you said "fine" when someone asked you how your meal at a restaurant or a room at a hotel was? Fine means passable, just okay. And that's not the standard of excellence we want for our work. Just okay is not okay.

What got you to where you are generally won't get you to where you want to be. As you and your organization progress and look to pursue new goals and aspirations, the strategies, skills, and mindset that have served you well in the past may need to be adjusted or expanded upon. Growth and progress often require you to step out of your comfort zone, learn new things, develop new skills, and adapt to changing circumstances.

It is vital to assess your current strengths and weaknesses, identify the areas where you need to improve, and be open to learning and acquiring new skills to reach new heights. It may involve seeking new experiences, challenging yourself, seeking guidance from others, and being willing to take risks or explore new paths.

As leaders, we must fight the tendency to get too comfortable. I have always been apprehensive about complacency, being comfortable and satisfied with the status quo. I aggressively avoid getting too comfortable, and I suggest that all leaders do the same.

My mantra is, "If it ain't broke, break it." Great leaders know change is good. They believe there are always things that can—and need to—improve. Change should be encouraged, expected, and celebrated. If we do not embrace change, we can easily and quickly settle into a rut that can devolve into uninspired inertia.

Leaders create a positive culture of change by actively championing and supporting it, significantly increasing the likelihood of success. Their influence, guidance, and commitment can create an environment where change is valued, encouraged, and seen as an opportunity for growth and improvement. Leaders should also allocate the critical resources for the training, tools, and support needed for individuals and teams to navigate change effectively.

Bring the idea of change front and center in your team's minds. Don't just analyze how change is handled when it is thrust upon your organization. Look for those who instigate and inspire change—the complainers who talk about what needs to change and the doers who make it happen. Incorporate change discussions into weekly meetings by asking people what they have changed, made better, improved, or done differently in their jobs. Evaluate everyone's flexibility and promote those who deal best with change.

Helping your team grow professionally and personally is all tied to change. If change doesn't happen, nothing grows, including the people and your organization.

A TINY MOMENT
"Fine" Is Never Enough

Vivian is the backbone of her company's software technology systems, ensuring everything runs smoothly and efficiently. Her colleagues value the stability she provides. On a particularly busy day, with multiple projects demanding her attention, she reluctantly joined a webinar she had signed up for. Multitasking through the session, she only half-listened—until a statement from the presenter grabbed her attention: "If you want to change things, you have to break things." This idea resonated with her deeply, making her realize that perhaps maintaining the status quo wasn't enough; maybe "fine" wasn't as good as it could be. When she returned to her office, the presenter's comment was fresh in her mind, so now everything around her seemed like a candidate for improvement. Is it currently working? (Mostly) yes. Could it be improved? Absolutely.

The very next day, Vivian found an opportunity to put her new perspective into action. During a meeting, Steve, a team member, presented his approach to a new web UX design project. His plan followed a familiar formula—one the team had successfully used before. Sensing the chance to challenge the status quo, Vivian spoke up. "Steve, your plan is solid, but what if we explored some unconventional ideas? How could we approach this differently?" Her question opened the door to fresh possibilities, encouraging the team to think beyond their usual methods.

In one Tiny Moment and with one simple question, Vivian changed Steve's mindset from staying on course to blazing a new path. While he was content with the original approach, he was awakened and reenergized by Vivian's request. The following week, he submitted designs that were a departure from the company's norm. His inspired work opened new and innovative avenues for the company's UX design, something they successfully integrated into their work moving forward.

Instead of maintaining existing systems, Vivian began to explore other areas in need of fresh solutions and encouraged her colleagues to think beyond the familiar. Vivian's newfound enthusiasm for change didn't go unnoticed, and soon her team began to view her as a leader who wasn't afraid to break away from the ordinary. She incorporated discussions about change into their weekly meetings, fostering an environment where innovation and improvement were not only valued but expected.

With one short sentence—"If you want to change things, you have to break things"—Vivian learned that being a leader means more than maintaining stability. It requires embracing change, inspiring others to do the same, and actively working toward a future where "fine" is replaced with "great." The mantra "If it ain't broke, break it" is now her guiding principle, reminding her and her team that innovation and progress are not only beneficial, but necessary for sustained success.

CHAPTER SIXTEEN

Create Urgency

URGENCY IS such a big part of who I am that I once earned the nickname "Itchy" because I always showed up ready to do things now. After all, the world is changing at an ever-increasing pace. My philosophy is, the faster things move around us, the faster we must move to keep up.

Great leaders keep their eye out for projects and tasks that can fall through the cracks and assign the proper urgency to them.

That's why urgency is essential for enacting change and making progress. As Lee Iacocca once said, "The speed of the boss is the speed of the team."

However, urgency is not just about speed; it's also about having purpose and focusing on what matters the most. It is a determination to focus on something now and every day that wins. It creates a priority for the need to change, emphasizes action, and overcomes any complacency that may be in place.

Pushing the team to work faster or do more than can reasonably be expected is not the same as creating urgency. You can burn out a team if the message is constantly barked, "You're not doing it fast enough." In these scenarios, just getting the work done can become more important than getting the work done right.

When introduced the right way, urgency conveys a sense of importance and vibrancy to the work. When skillfully embraced, urgency does not equate to stress, but rather, is a motivated mindset that empowers teams to get started and to prioritize tasks efficiently.

Deadlines are an obvious tool for creating urgency, but how they are implemented defines the difference between a manager and a leader. A manager shares a deadline by whatever means the organization uses, something as simple as a list or as involved as production software. Either way, the manager says, "This is what needs to be done and this is the due date." And then the manager walks away.

A leader might start from the same place, but instead of walking away, she will make sure the team has questions answered and needs met to reach this goal. Additionally, she might encourage the team members to create their own sense of urgency through self-created deadlines for accomplishing the task-required deliverable.

But even more importantly, great leaders keep their eye out for projects and tasks that can fall through the cracks and assign the proper urgency to them. Sometimes people don't see the big picture in the same way as you do and, as a result, they don't understand how important it is that all the pieces fit together.

In his book *A Sense of Urgency*, Harvard Business School professor John Kotter underscores the critical importance of combating complacency and fostering true urgency. He writes, "Complacency is pervasive, in part because it simply is not seen, even by many smart, experienced, and sophisticated people." Kotter highlights how organizations often mistake frenetic activity for genuine urgency, noting that such false urgency "is more distracting than useful" and can even be detrimental. True urgency, he explains, is driven by a deep determination to act on critical issues now, ensuring meaningful progress each day.[1]

Without urgency, momentum stalls, making it hard to sustain a competitive edge. To keep your organization moving forward, ensure that urgency remains a constant under your leadership. It's this driving force that pushes individuals and teams out of their comfort zones, sparking the innovation and progress needed for lasting change. Keep urgency alive, and you'll maintain the momentum that fuels growth and success.

A TINY MOMENT

Sparking Action in a World That Won't Wait

When artificial intelligence (AI) began to emerge, marketing companies were trying to catch up like all other industries. Our agency is a busy place, so while everyone was interested, our progress with harnessing the power of AI wasn't moving along like it needed to.

Eventually, I started to become uneasy. We were learning and making some progress, but we needed to be faster to keep up. I knew that just talking about AI wasn't going to be enough. So I gathered the senior leadership group for a meeting. This gathering became a Tiny Moment in reinforcing that it was up to us as leaders to create the necessary urgency to get the ball rolling.

We decided to create an internal agency, the "AI Institute." Everyone was asked to explore and bring valuable resources, knowledge, and ideas to the organization. We designed the initiative to ensure that every team member could contribute to our collective understanding and application of AI. By making it a team effort, we aimed to accelerate our learning curve and implementation.

To facilitate this, we used our online forum platform to share articles and other information and compile a repository of AI knowledge that is easily accessible to everyone in the agency. We also held lunch-and-learn sessions, where team members could present their findings and discuss new AI developments. These sessions fostered a collaborative learning environment and kept the momentum going.

In addition to these formal initiatives, we made a point to keep AI at top of mind by talking about it with each other on a regular basis. Casual conversations about AI became common, whether in meetings, during coffee breaks, or via internal messaging. This constant dialogue helped to normalize AI within our agency culture and encouraged everyone to think about how we could integrate it with our work.

Soon, our awareness of AI and how it could help us began to get baked into our daily operations. We created urgency by building a consciousness and new level of awareness that had not been there before. This heightened focus on AI began to manifest in our projects and strategies. We started to see real-world applications of AI in our campaigns, from advanced data analysis to personalized marketing efforts.

Our AI Institute became a hub of innovation, driving us to experiment with new technologies and approaches. The collective knowledge we amassed empowered us to stay ahead of the curve and leverage AI to its fullest potential. It also fostered a sense of pride and accomplishment within the team, as everyone contributed to our AI journey.

This initiative highlighted the importance of proactive leadership and the need to foster a culture of continuous learning. By taking decisive action and creating a structured approach to AI education, we were able to transform a potential weakness into a significant strength. The Tiny Moment of gathering the senior leadership to address our AI strategy proved to be a pivotal point in our agency's evolution.

In the end, our commitment to embracing AI not only enhanced our capabilities but also solidified our position as an innovative and forward-thinking agency. This experience taught us that staying ahead requires not just interest but a concerted effort and a shared sense of urgency.

CHAPTER SEVENTEEN

The Worst Decision Is No Decision

MAKING BUSINESS decisions can be difficult. And risky. The best course is not always clear. There is always more than one solution that can be right. You may not have all the facts and information you need. Things can always go wrong.

When you take too long to make a decision, you run the risk of letting opportunities pass you by.

Because of these and other reasons, many people avoid making decisions and fall into decision paralysis. Maybe they're waiting for someone else to decide so they don't have to be responsible. Maybe they're hoping the "what if" will be avoided through inaction. Maybe they're waiting for divine intervention to resolve the situation. These are not the thoughts and actions of a leader.

When you devote less time to "maybe," you get more time for action. One thing I have never heard anyone say after taking action on a tricky situation is, "I wish I had waited longer."

How others perceive your decision-making can make or break you as a leader. Outside advice, suggestions, and feedback may be encouraged and welcomed, but in the end, someone must make the call—and that somebody is you. Leaders must not be afraid to speak their minds.

Effective leaders weigh ideas like shoppers thump melons to test for ripeness. They assess opportunities to see if they are ripe for investment, even when they cannot see inside. They are not afraid to take calculated risks because they understand when to move swiftly with the available information and when to take more time and gather additional data. While more data can be desirable, the process of gathering it can sometimes be time-consuming, drawing focus away from the overall vision and critical insights.

The high wire that influential leaders must walk is winning minds, but also sometimes making unpopular decisions—or decisions that people do not understand.

Leaders who have developed the courage to make decisions realize that most are not life-altering on their own and almost all of them can be changed later. When you make a decision and move forward, you at least reveal whether the decision was right and whether to backtrack or continue. Develop a "Plan B" with ways to backtrack and correct course if necessary.

Time spent over-contemplating is wasted time. When you take too long to make a decision, you run the risk of letting opportunities pass you by.

Theodore Roosevelt reportedly said, "In any moment of decision, the best thing you can do is the right thing, the next best thing is the wrong thing, and the worst thing you can do is nothing."[1] Just like the squirrel that runs in front of your car and can't decide what to do, indecision can kill you.

In this book, I talk a lot about challenging those around you to be proactive and exhibit leadership qualities. If leaders do their job well, decision-making is "distributed" and gridlock dissipates. Such leaders create others who are comfortable making decisions and a truly effective organization evolves. It's the circle of life!

A TINY MOMENT

Decide on a Course Before It's Too Late

When news of the Covid-19 pandemic started to break, the world was gripped with uncertainty. It was impossible to know what to do in such unfamiliar territory. No one had any experience with such a situation, and we were all scrambling to figure it out on our own. The news updates were constantly shifting, and it was impossible to know what the best decision would be for my marketing business. Our staff members were used to working closely together in the office, and our relationships with our clients were equally hands-on.

I watched and listened to other leaders trying to figure out the best next steps. In the middle of the madness, I heard a podcast on my way into the office. The conversation was about decision-making and the guest speaker said, "When listening to someone talk about how they navigated a difficult business situation and arrived at a direction to take, you never hear them say, 'I wish I had taken longer to make that decision.'"

The timing for me to hear this was ideal. It inspired me to stop waiting for the passage of time or for something unknown to happen to get on with the decisions I needed to make. It is my company, my team, my clients, my responsibility. Though sending everyone to work from home and (temporarily) reducing our staff to keep the company afloat were all big swings, the Tiny Moment was hearing that podcast and taking ownership of the need to make a decision and to take a stand. People depended on me to make decisions—even in the middle of great uncertainty. As the captain of a ship facing a storm, my crew couldn't focus until I gave clear directions. I couldn't know exactly how things would turn out at the time, but only after a decision was made could we start to find our way.

CHAPTER EIGHTEEN

Unmet Expectations Are the Source of Conflict

WE LIVE our lives full of expectations: Personal and professional. Big and small. Positive and negative.

Remember this in your own life: Expectations created are expectations expected.

Think about how expectations make you feel. There is contemplation and foresight. Maybe high hopes, perhaps dread. Whatever the feeling evoked by expectations, you can be sure of one thing: They create emotion and anticipation. And whenever people have emotion and anticipation, the stakes are high.

According to William Shakespeare, "Expectation is at the root of all heartache."

Why such a bleak view? Human beings tend to pin their hopes on expectations being fulfilled and, as a result, being happy. That can work well when we have realistic expectations and take the necessary steps toward meeting them. For instance, a particular meal at our favorite restaurant consistently pleases us. Therefore, we expect to be happy after a meal there; as a rule, we are (almost always, anyway).

The problem occurs when we expect something to happen, and it doesn't.

The result is disappointment, frustration, even anger. We had high hopes, and they were dashed. I'm sure you can think of many examples of this happening in your life. Maybe it was hope for a new job, a date, or a vacation that didn't materialize.

Remember this in your own life: Expectations created are expectations expected, whether with your significant other, an employee, or a client. Most importantly, remember that unmet expectations create conflict.

Poor communication is most often the source of unmet expectations. If you do not clearly explain what you expect from them, you leave it up to your employees to fill in the blanks. All too often, the outcome they envision is significantly better than the reality. So naturally, they are disappointed and possibly angry when expectations and reality clash. Things generally don't go well from there.

As leaders, we must strive to set clear expectations for those around us. First, make sure you are clear in your mind about what you expect. Discuss fully and ask a lot of questions. Get an agreement and commitment. Build a roadmap together, based as much as possible on goals and measures of success. And by all means, write them down!

Some say that disappointment over unmet expectations is part of the human condition, and we are destined to suffer from it. However, unmet expectations can be curtailed and managed with a conscious and mature approach. Being clear and communicating our expectations can strengthen us and make us better leaders and employees.

A TINY MOMENT
Don't Let It Go

Shelley, a woman I know who works at a small film production company, always seems to thrive under pressure. However, the demands of her job are relentless. She constantly juggles tight schedules, high creative expectations, and clients' vivid visions, all of which can push her to her limits. One day, she found herself in the eye of a storm when a client erupted in rage over a project they believed missed the mark entirely.

Shelley was understandably troubled by the client's dissatisfaction. She pored over the agreements, trying to pinpoint where things had gone wrong. She soon realized that vague explanations and gray areas had created a breeding ground for misinterpretation. She dug deep into what had gone wrong, uncovering a web of assumptions and conflicting expectations. Both parties believed they were in the right, highlighting just how murky the communication had been.

It would have been easy to blame the client, but Shelley had heard that narrative too many times. Instead, she saw this painful experience as a chance to learn and grow. Determined to prevent future misunderstandings, Shelley took proactive steps. She had open, honest conversations with her team and the client, clarifying every detail and using explicit language. She made sure everyone involved had a realistic understanding of what was possible within the given constraints.

This change in approach came from a Tiny Moment of inspiration, a decision to untangle the miscommunication rather than let it fester. It showed Shelley's unwavering resolve to ensure smoother collaborations in the future. Her journey is a powerful reminder that genuine effort and clear communication are essential in overcoming the challenges of creative work.

CHAPTER NINETEEN

Be a Role Model of Character and Ethics

ONE LEADERSHIP attribute is so critical that those who don't have it can disqualify themselves from the role. That attribute is integrity.

People may not consciously recognize integrity, but they will undoubtedly notice a lack of it.

Integrity is grounded in basic honesty, positive values, and sound character. Trust is built upon it. And without it, leaders cannot lead.

Integrity is the strength and willingness to be direct with others. It is a decision you make to stand on inherently good principles, always striving to do what you know in your heart is the right thing. True integrity takes commitment and resolve, and it is the very foundation upon which leaders build successful businesses.

The Greek philosopher Heraclitus once said, "Character is destiny." Moral integrity shapes your future. If you want to be a leader, you need trust; if you want trust, you must demonstrate that you are a person of character. Aristotle postulated that good character is one of the most important means of persuasion. Who are we to argue with Heraclitus and Aristotle?

When you compromise on values, ethics, and honesty, you risk losing the respect and trust of those who follow you. People inside the organization will respond to what they see and feel from you, withholding their trust and being less transparent. No one wants to work for, or with, someone they don't trust.

People rarely rise above their leader's level of morality and ethics. As I said earlier, you are a role model. The world needs role models. It's how each generation learns how they will live their lives. As leaders, providing an example for others to follow is both a responsibility and an opportunity.

Great leaders realize it is their responsibility to ensure their values and beliefs are put into practice within the organization. This can require taking the moral and ethical high road in ways that others might find challenging to accept, such as turning down the opportunity to gain profit when the tactics don't align with your values. Great leaders make decisions for the right reasons, not merely because they are expedient, convenient, or profitable.

Leadership is complicated and can involve morally gray areas that are difficult to navigate if you don't approach them with a pre-established value system. Having character and ethics means doing what is right when no one is watching and without expectation of acknowledgment. People may not consciously recognize integrity, but they will undoubtedly notice a lack of it.

Kareem Abdul-Jabbar is credited as having said, "I try to do the right thing at the right time. They may just be little things, but usually they make the difference between winning and losing."

Wise words from a man who knows a thing or two about winning.

A TINY MOMENT
Live the Truth

Sometimes a Tiny Moment is found in an example of what NOT to do.

Throughout my career, I've had the privilege of working with diverse personalities spanning all levels of the corporate hierarchy. From dishwashers to CEOs, I've encountered the full spectrum of professional backgrounds.

These interactions have gifted me a unique perspective on character and ethics in leadership.

One small but impactful encounter remains etched in my memory. It took place during a conversation with Joy, a local political official with considerable influence and power. She mentioned to me that Mike, a local business leader, had expressed a desire to meet with me to resolve an issue of local importance. However, a few days later, when I ran into Mike and mentioned the meeting, he said, "Yes, Joy thought it would be a good idea for us to get together."

If Joy wanted the meeting, why hadn't she been forthright about it? What motivations lay hidden behind the facade of deception in trying to make me think Mike—and not Joy—was calling for the meeting? In reality, the meeting was to further Joy's agenda, and she was camouflaging it by saying Mike wanted to meet. Unfortunately for her, I caught on to her disingenuous approach.

At first glance, this may appear to be a minor incident unworthy of extensive contemplation. Yet, the encounter had a lasting impact on me. Her untruth had sown a seed of doubt. This tiny act of dishonesty had chipped away at Joy's integrity and had blemished the foundation of trust.

The experience served as a poignant reminder that even the smallest acts of dishonesty can erode the integrity of a leader. Joy's failure to be transparent had permanently undermined her credibility and trustworthiness in my eyes. This small error underscores that honesty, transparency, and forthrightness are not to be taken lightly. A leader's character and ethics should shine just as brightly as their achievements because it is in these seemingly minor moments that outstanding leadership shows its true essence.

Motivational speaker Kenneth H. Blanchard said it best: "Honesty is telling the truth to ourselves and others. Integrity is living that truth."[1]

Approach all interactions with an unwavering commitment to honesty and integrity. Understand that in the realm of business, where trust is the lifeblood of relationships, even a tiny white lie could tip the scales and alter the perception of your character and your capacity to lead effectively.

CHAPTER TWENTY

True Character Is Revealed in Adversity

ANYONE CAN be positive and strong when things are going well. That's easy. It's when things don't go well that we see one's true personality and temperament.

As Warren Buffett has written in his many letters to company shareholders over the years, "you only find out who is swimming naked when the tide goes out."[1]

Building the type of character that confidently leads through adversity takes experience, practice, and intentionality.

Character is the set of qualities that display who we really are on the inside. It is about how we respond to the events and circumstances in our lives—both good and bad. Sure, the words we speak are important, but talk can be cheap, and anyone can say anything. Character is defined by what we do, how we act, and the way we lead when it matters the most, such as when the business is struggling, when the team loses an emotional game, or when misfortune shows up at our doorstep. During these times, people look to their leaders for comfort, confidence, and guidance.

This is where the idea that "pressure is a privilege" comes into play.

When you're under pressure, it means you're in a position of significance, where your actions truly matter. Rather than viewing pressure as a burden, it should be embraced as an opportunity to demonstrate leadership, resilience, and strength of character. Those who thrive under pressure not only rise to the occasion but also inspire others to do the same.

We often mask the true nature of what is inside us. However, it is difficult (perhaps impossible) to put on that mask during challenging circumstances. Difficult times reveal our true colors, and what is exposed can be enlightening: It may be great leadership and a strong constitution or something more hesitant, unglued, and powerless. Life's pressure, stress, and adversity push what is inside us to the surface. It is a mirror that reflects who we really are and whether our response mechanisms are mature or immature.

Some say that suffering produces character. While it is admittedly challenging, try to identify and be thankful for opportunities to build character. Be aware and make note of your emotions and how you respond when things don't go your way. What does your behavior reveal about the content of your character? What does the first thought that comes to mind say about you and your leadership qualities?

Building the type of character that confidently leads through adversity takes experience, practice, and intentionality. One thing is for sure: You'll have plenty of opportunity, because in life there's always another storm brewing. And that can be a fantastic opportunity for you to be the one who steps up, not back, when skillful and inspiring leadership is needed most.

American writer Frank A. Clark once said, "If you can find a path with no obstacles, it probably doesn't lead anywhere." The true test and leading indicator of success will be how our leaders handle these obstacles and whether they confidently light the path for moving forward.

A TINY MOMENT
Take a Beat Before You React

We once lost a big client unexpectedly over a conference call. We went into the call thinking we were going over the plans for the next year, which would generate a lot of income for our company, and we left the call without the client because they had decided to take the work elsewhere. When we got off the call, you could feel the tension in the room. Everyone waited to see my response.

In a book dedicated to Tiny Moments, the reality is that the tiniest moment is what happens in your head in the split second before you respond to any situation. I knew they were watching me, and though I was screaming on the inside, I took a deep breath, remained extremely calm, and invited everyone to talk about what had happened, what we had missed, and how we could learn from it as a team moving forward. Above all else, I knew I had to create a safe place for adversity because if I had followed through on my initial reaction and exploded, I would have created an environment of fear where people would potentially hide difficult or bad news in the future. This environment would be far more damaging in the long run than losing one single account.

Being mindful and careful in the face of adversity doesn't mean all is forgiven and there are no consequences, but it inspires others to face challenges with a solutionist mentality rather than fear. When the dust settled, some changes were made, but those decisions came from a place of clarity and consideration rather than pointing fingers on the spot. Rash and brutal actions made publicly are nearly impossible to retract. Your character as a leader is more important than any one client's decision.

Remember, everyone is watching you and how you react to issues and situations. Always.

CHAPTER TWENTY-ONE

Be Mindful of Your Power

THE PARADOX of power is that the qualities that help individuals gain leadership positions often vanish once they rise to power. Instead of being polite, honest, and outgoing, they become impulsive, reckless, and rude.

Arrogant leaders aren't leaders at all; they're managers who bully.

According to psychologists, authority "makes us less sympathetic to the concerns and emotions of others."[1]

Here's the problem: Power activates the reward circuitry in the brain and creates an addictive "high." Power boosts our testosterone, increasing the supply of the neurotransmitter dopamine, the so-called feel-good hormone, to the brain's reward system. According to Ian Robertson, professor of psychology at Trinity College in Dublin, power has similar effects as cocaine, which also produces dopamine.[2] We feel like we can do almost anything, and we may become arrogant and impatient. This is when feeling powerful leads to abusing power and ultimately to self-destruction.

The dynamics of power can profoundly influence how we think. When we climb the ladder of status, our inner self gets warped and our natural sympathy for others fades. Instead of fretting about the effects of our actions, we just go ahead and act. Power and influence can make us believe we are invincible—that we do not need to be held accountable.

A video study of people eating conducted by Dacher Keltner, a professor of psychology at Cal Berkeley, showed that people in power are more likely to eat with their mouths open and their lips smacking.[3] They are the ones who grab the last cookie on the plate. An ugly picture, right? Unfortunately, power can be blind.

Throughout history, power has corrupted countless leaders. People like Josef Stalin, Vladimir Putin, Slobodan Milosevic, Saddam Hussein, and so many others have all committed shameful actions, either drunk on power or driven by greed, or, more likely, both. Unchecked authority and the desire for control can cause people to act in incomprehensible ways.

Arrogant leaders aren't leaders at all; they're managers who bully. You may be able to scare someone into doing something, but you cannot force respect, admiration, trust, and loyalty.

The dangers related to a leader's character are significant, underscoring the need for leaders to approach their roles with a healthy degree of caution. They must recognize the profound impact their character has on organizational culture and employee morale, emphasizing the importance of self-reflection and a commitment to ethical conduct to avoid these potential pitfalls.

Abraham Lincoln once said, "If you want to test a man's character, give him power." The world would be a better place if more leaders passed that test.

A TINY MOMENT
The Power to Know When to Stay Quiet

Influenced by the sense of self-importance that power can create, you may feel you should be involved in everything that goes on in your office. However, sometimes you will find yourself in a meeting that would be better without your presence.

I recall a series of meetings during which I was very engaged in conversations about plans to take our content creation offerings into new areas, genres, and platforms. The first meeting, which focused on strategic and deliverable-driven aspects, was of great interest to me, and I thought I could make a positive difference in this space.

The next meeting was creative-focused, and I was quieter. Sure, I like to play in that sandbox, but there were a lot of very creative people in the room. In fact, I told a couple of team leads later that I was biting through my lip to keep my mouth shut. They were tossing around all kinds of ideas, many of which were not great, but that's the fun part of the creative process. I own a creative agency but did not rise through the ranks as a creative myself, so I have great respect for approaches different from mine.

If I had led with my power in this scenario, it would have disrupted the flow necessary to be successful. I certainly am forceful in some situations, but not all. Being mindful of power comes into play when choosing between the two. This was not my meeting to control, so I turned my power toward keeping my mouth shut.

You lose power when you abuse it, so stay aware of how, when, and why you use it. This Tiny Moment of in-the-moment self-reflection can create the difference between leadership and damage.

CHAPTER TWENTY-TWO

Care + Confrontation = Carefrontation

P ICTURE THIS: You're at work, and someone does something that really annoys you. In fact, you find what this person has done to be counterproductive to mutual respect, group camaraderie, and ultimately, team success. This person's actions do not

Teach those around you to avoid gossip and damaged relationships by practicing carefrontation and having direct, honest, and caring conversations.

live up to the core values and standards that your company has set for itself and its employees.

You have two choices: On one hand, you can choose to not say anything to cause conflict and damage relationships. Or you could be a bit braver and have a conversation with that person. Let's picture how the latter option plays out.

Imagine you're a team leader, and you notice that some misguided behavior of a particular team member is negatively affecting team morale and the quality of work. You choose a private setting and the right timing for an uninterrupted conversation. You begin the conversation by expressing your genuine concern for both individual and team success. You acknowledge that challenges are natural and part of growth and that your goal is to address these challenges collaboratively. Using specific examples, you share your observations. You emphasize that your intention is not to assign blame or be negative but to collectively find ways to improve. You actively listen without interruption, showing that you value their input and understand their viewpoints. Together, you agree on action steps for the future.

Never allow conflict to smolder. It is very destructive to do so. Nip it in the bud by addressing the situation without delay. (See chapter 13.) Shying away from conflict and being reluctant to address issues lays the groundwork for damage to the organization.

Knowing how to confront conflict respectfully is key to success for leaders and employees. If you let conflict, or even annoyances, smolder, hoping they will resolve themselves, you only sweep the flames under the table. That will eventually burn the table down, resulting in resentment that only makes things worse.

"Carefrontation" blends "care" and "confrontation," suggesting a compassionate and thoughtful approach to addressing difficult or challenging situations. When you practice carefrontation, you create an environment where difficult conversations are approached with empathy, respect, and a focus on positive outcomes. This approach not only resolves issues but also contributes to personal and organizational growth.

By practicing carefrontation in this scenario, you've addressed a sensitive issue with empathy and opened a space for honest dialogue. While it may be a bit difficult at the outset, in the end, that team member recognizes and appreciates the transparent opportunity for personal growth and improvement. Many people avoid confrontation at all costs, sometimes to the detriment of their well-being and peace of mind. But when you learn to address issues with care and compassion, everyone can learn and grow.

Be clear on the facts from your point of view and then present them in a way that doesn't feel like an attack. Listen to and respect contradicting perceptions and move things toward a sensible resolution. Debate is welcome and an important part of action. If it becomes heated, it's usually because emotions are moving front and center—and that helps no one.

As the leader, it is incumbent on you to commit to carefrontation, become proficient at it, and—very importantly—integrate it into your company culture. If not taught and encouraged otherwise, team members often resort to talking to others in the office about the situation rather than addressing it directly with the person in question. This can quickly deteriorate into office gossip and result in damaged chemistry. Teach those around you to avoid gossip and damaged relationships by practicing carefrontation and having direct, honest, and caring conversations.

I once heard someone proudly say his company avoids difficult conversations with each other because they have a "get-along" culture. My reaction to this is to question how a company can possibly have a "get-along" culture if they aren't willing to openly talk about issues that arise. In fact, the ONLY way to get along is to have what might be considered difficult conversations that are the key to honest interaction, a healthy environment, and positive camaraderie.

A TINY MOMENT
The Power of Direct Communication

Susan worked for me as a promotions manager during my pro sports team days. Unfortunately, she tended to say things behind people's backs instead of addressing issues directly. If someone did something that annoyed her, she was more likely to vent her frustrations to a colleague rather than confront the person responsible. This tendency created a culture of gossip and unresolved tension within the team.

One incident stands out vividly in my memory. I saw Susan was visibly upset about a coworker's behavior. The tension was palpable, and the office environment was becoming increasingly uncomfortable. I decided it was time to intervene and help Susan address the issue constructively.

I went into her office and closed the door behind me. Susan was clearly surprised by my unexpected visit. I could see the uncertainty in her eyes. "Susan," I began gently, "I know you're upset about what happened, and

I understand why. But I think it's important that you talk to the person directly about how you feel."

Susan looked down at her desk, avoiding eye contact. "I don't know if I can," she admitted. "What if they get angry or defensive?"

I sat down across from her and leaned forward, trying to convey my support and encouragement. "I understand that it can be intimidating," I said, "but avoiding the conversation only makes things worse. The person may not even realize they're doing something that bothers you. By talking to them, you give them a chance to understand your perspective and make changes."

Susan remained silent for a moment, contemplating my words. I could see she was wrestling with her fear of confrontation and the desire to resolve the issue. "I call it a 'carefrontation,'" I added. "It's about approaching the conversation with care and respect, not as an attack. You want to clear the air and let the person know how you feel, but you also want to do it in a way that fosters understanding and cooperation."

"Carefrontation," she repeated. "I like that."

I smiled, sensing a breakthrough. "Exactly. You're not just confronting them; you're showing that you care enough about the relationship and the team's harmony to have an honest conversation."

We spent the next few minutes discussing how she could approach the conversation, role-playing different scenarios and possible responses. Susan started to feel more confident, realizing that she had the tools and support to handle the situation effectively.

A few days later, Susan came to my office with a smile on her face. "I did it," she said proudly. "I talked to them, and it went really well. They didn't even realize their behavior was bothering me. We had a good discussion, and things have been much better since then."

Encouraging Susan to engage in carefrontation was a Tiny Moment that not only resolved the immediate issue but also instilled in her a valuable skill that would serve her well throughout her career. The experience reinforced the importance of direct communication and the positive impact it can have on team dynamics.

CHAPTER TWENTY-THREE

The Keanu Quotient

THERE ARE many charity events every year that garner the support of actors, singers, and athletes. They walk red carpets in extraordinary fashion to raise awareness for causes that matter to them. There's no denying how impressive it can be to see the vast amounts of

Before we can lead others and expect a certain presence from them, we need to first look at ourselves and be the best we can be.

money they raise and donate to help humanity. But the organizations that benefit from these grandiose events are often overshadowed by the pomp and circumstance of superstardom.

Keanu Reeves is an outlier in Hollywood. While some may easily write him off as a weird hippie actor with an odd name, his career mixes mainstream blockbusters with arthouse flicks. What's fascinating about Keanu's approach to celebrity is his complete disregard for many of the nuances that usually define celebrities. He's rarely on the red carpet unless it's for one of his films, and his personal life is mostly quiet and out of the tabloids. This reserved nature is particularly refreshing in an industry that often thrives on excess and spectacle.

Reeves is often described by those who've worked with him and fans who've met him as a person of profound humility and kindness. Unlike many celebrities who use their fame as a platform to elevate their charitable endeavors, Reeves takes a quieter and more personal approach, finding joy in connecting with others in meaningful ways. His private foundation, which donates to children's hospitals and cancer research, remains anonymous because he doesn't seek personal accolades. Similarly, his everyday gestures—like giving up his subway seat or helping passengers after a flight emergency—showcase how he uses his influence to improve the lives of others without fanfare. For Reeves, the act of helping others is its own reward, done without the need for recognition or fanfare.

His kindness extends beyond his interactions with the public. On set, he's known for valuing every contributor, from stuntmen to costume designers. After the Matrix sequels, Reeves gifted Harley-Davidson motorcycles to a dozen stuntmen as a gesture of gratitude for their efforts. He has also taken pay cuts on several films to ensure that other members of the crew were compensated fairly. These acts highlight a critical leadership principle: Lifting others up often requires stepping back from the spotlight. Reeves demonstrates that true leadership comes from a willingness to support and elevate those around you, creating an environment of mutual respect and shared success.

None of the stories about Keanu Reeves are public because he talked about them. We only know about them because others talked about and documented their exchanges with him. His character and compassion are evident, and there's no need to try to second-guess his motives. As he is commonly held as having said, "The simple act of paying attention can take you a long way."

Before we can lead others and expect a certain presence from them, we need to first look at ourselves and be the best we can be. All of us would be closer to our best with some Keanu Reeves mixed in. His ability to remain humble despite his immense success, coupled with his resilience in the face of personal challenges, serves as a powerful example for leaders navigating the complexities of organizations.

This authentic and compassionate approach can only foster positive relationships and an environment in which individuals feel valued and motivated. Making this part of your personal brand as a leader will instill a sense of trust and loyalty among your team members and foster a positive organizational climate.

In the realm of leadership, a paramount quality to emulate from Keanu Reeves is the ability to give selflessly without seeking recognition. This selflessness illustrates how seemingly small actions can leave an indelible mark on those we lead.

A TINY MOMENT
It Doesn't Require Flash to Shine

When a high-profile tech company in our area elevated a friend of mine to the position of CEO, she found herself thrust into the spotlight. Amelia's predecessor had been known for somewhat flashy displays of success, often drawing public attention with an assertive presence. As Amelia stepped into her new role, she felt that such showmanship didn't resonate with her personal core beliefs. At first it felt necessary to gain awareness, but she decided to test the waters by using a different approach.

At her first industry conference as CEO, instead of walking around "on the red carpet," Amelia chose a more subdued approach. She avoided the extravagance of the limelight and instead engaged in genuine conversations, setting a tone of approachability and authenticity. This departure from her predecessor's style was a subtle signal of a leadership style that focused on substance rather than showmanship.

As her tenure unfolded, Amelia continued to defy expectations. During a critical project, she worked side by side with her team, demonstrating a hands-on approach that inspired them. When Amelia had to make a grand announcement to the media, something about it felt inauthentic. Coincidentally, she had read an article mentioning Keanu Reeves's quiet generosity on a recent flight, which inspired Amelia to express her gratitude for the company's success with personalized notes to every team member.

The press announcement still happened, but only after she made the Tiny Moment decision first to thank her team. Her leadership was defined by a commitment to authenticity and a genuine connection with her team, surprising those who expected a more ostentatious display from the CEO's office. In this unexpected turn of events, Amelia emerged as a leader who valued results over flash, proving that authentic leadership often speaks louder in actions than in extravagant displays.

CHAPTER TWENTY-FOUR

Birds of a Feather Flock Together

I HAVE LONG led my organizations with the standard that everyone must be an A-player or on the way to becoming one. Here's what I expect out of A-players:

Confucius said, "If you are the smartest person in the room, then you are in the wrong room."

- Reflect our core values

- Be a learner

- Have passion

- Always bring your best

- Be a self-starter

- Deliver positive energy

- Practice "carefrontation"

- Work toward high efficiency

- Contribute to our culture

- Ask questions

A-players are motivated to achieve at an elevated level when surrounded by those who also perform at a higher level. They become inspired and want to do well to match the excellence around them. They don't want to let their very capable colleagues down but instead move the work forward in a positive way.

On the flip side, A-players get frustrated when they work with subpar colleagues; they find it demotivating. They feel when not everyone is rowing in the same direction, it diminishes the value of their hard work. So, not only do the non-A-players underperform, but they also drag others down with them. That's no way to run a railroad, as an old idiom proclaims.

Companies win when they clearly and meaningfully distinguish between top and bottom performers and then cultivate strength in the latter. Just as companies invest their resources into the businesses or product lines with the highest ROI, winning leaders invest in people where the payback is highest.

Differentiation is when we assess employees, separate them into categories according to their performance, and act on that distinction. It is the fairest and kindest way to operate. And ultimately, it makes winners out of everyone.

The concept of the "law of attraction" goes back to Confucius in the sixth century BC, who wrote, "If you are the smartest person in the room, then you are in the wrong room."

Good parents pay attention to who their kids hang out with and worry about them falling in with the wrong crowd. That's because their friends have an enormous influence on how they view the world, the expectations they have of themselves, and how they behave. Proximity is power. Those you spend the most time with will influence who you eventually become, so you must surround yourself with people who are challenging and inspiring.

Great leaders use proximity to their advantage. In the words of Tony Robbins, "If we surround ourselves with people who are successful, who are forward-moving, who are positive, who are focused on producing results, who support us, it will challenge us to be more and do more and share more. If you can surround yourself with people who will never let you settle for less than you can be, you have the greatest gift that anyone can hope for."[1]

"Addition by Subtraction" is a concept embraced by Jack Welch. The well-regarded former chairman and CEO of General Electric believed that in all organizations, the top 20 percent are the stars, the middle 70 percent are valuable in terms of their skills, energy, and commitment, and the bottom 10 percent must go.[2]

Companies win when they make a clear and meaningful distinction between top and bottom performers and when they cultivate the strong and cull the weak. We must identify and then develop those in the middle 70 percent who have the potential to move up. Challenge and keep them engaged through training, positive feedback, and goal setting. One of the best things about dealing with the bottom 10 percent is that they often go on to successful careers in other fields or companies. This concept is like the playground—those not good at sports do something else.

A TINY MOMENT
Separating the Wheat from the Chaff

I have always believed that excellence begets excellence. However, early in my career, I had yet to develop the techniques and practices needed to foster this environment.

In a transformational moment of my career, initiated by a tiny but impactful moment, I shifted my leadership perspective from merely expecting A-player behavior to taking a more active role in ensuring that accountability was in place.

There was a time when my team struggled to deliver consistently exceptional work within the time frame allotted. In one Tiny Moment, I accepted the realization that my approach of simply expecting excellence without providing the necessary support and structure was failing us. Acting on this realization, I set up individual meetings with each team member to understand their challenges. During these conversations, along with more purposeful ongoing observations, I validated where the weak links were. I introduced performance improvement plans for these individuals and was fair to them, but I did not hesitate to let them go if and when it became clear they just weren't a good fit. It is always difficult to let someone go, but, when necessary, I know I have to do it without delay.

By addressing the personnel issues and setting up regular check-ins to confirm A-player performance, I saw a remarkable improvement in their work and morale. This approach allowed me to align the team's goals and capabilities better, fostering a more accountable and motivated work environment. In doing so, through the commitment to surround myself and my team with individuals who embodied the traits of A-players, I embraced the power of the law of attraction and proximity. This intentional approach had a ripple effect, with team members influencing each other positively.

Recognizing the importance of "Addition by Subtraction," I identified areas for improvement within the team. Through thoughtful coaching and mentorship, I worked with the middle 70 percent, nurturing their potential and guiding them toward upward growth. Simultaneously, I recognized the importance of letting go of those in the bottom 10 percent, understanding that it was an essential step in the pursuit of organizational excellence.

As a result of my commitment to differentiation and cultivation, the team flourished. The A-players found renewed motivation, feeding off each other's positive energy. The middle 70 percent responded to the challenge and engagement, evolving into increasingly valuable contributors. Many of those in the bottom 10 percent, redirected toward more suitable paths, went on to succeed in different endeavors. This experience exemplified to me the transformative impact that a shift in behavior can have on an entire team, creating a culture where everyone is expected to be a winner.

CHAPTER TWENTY-FIVE

Win Hearts to Win Minds

MANAGERS OFTEN tell others what to do without regard to whether people understand the purpose of the assignment or how they feel about it. In this scenario, the message is basically, "This

Great leaders don't rule. They influence behavior by winning hearts and minds.

needs to get done, so do it." Effective leaders deliver the same directive in a way that team members understand and respect.

Great leaders don't rule. They influence behavior by winning hearts and minds.

This applies to specific tasks as well as more significant goals. It can become particularly challenging if the assignment disrupts "business as usual." Even if "the way we've always done it" is difficult or unnecessarily time-consuming, employees will meet workflow changes with apprehension if they're unknown.

For instance, a more streamlined bookkeeping system may feel like a risk to an accountant's job security. If the data entry that filled their days is now automated, they may think a machine will replace them. However, if they understand that the change will create positive results for them, they will be 100 percent on board. Only by connecting with them emotionally and intellectually can you win their trust and loyalty.

Noted essayist John Burroughs once said, "When you bait your hook with your heart, the fish always bite."[1] Heeding this advice using leadership, vision, and direction will supercharge your ability to coalesce people and influence them to do great things.

Take these steps to win hearts and minds:

1. Begin with empathy.

2. Describe a universally relevant situation.

3. Take a moment to understand and consider the various perspectives.

4. Establish common ground among the involved parties.

5. Share your expertise, emphasizing personal experiences and analysis.

6. Support your position with data, research, and expert opinions.

7. Discuss the tangible benefits of the proposed ideas or changes.

Once you've shared the plan and the rationale, listen to everyone's questions and concerns. Be open to suggestions as long as they move things forward. Ultimately, leaders must make decisions in the best interest of the company. Sometimes, an idea won't move forward for a variety of reasons. Evaluate and explain the final decisions so that even if things must move in a different direction, the team has the information and isn't left feeling like their suggestions were a waste of time.

It is not hard to imagine the benefit of moving forward with people who understand and agree with the direction they are heading as opposed to those who are doing something because you told them to do it.

There's a business adage that leadership is like a spaghetti noodle: You can pull it along fairly easily, but you can't push it.

A TINY MOMENT

From Headstrong to Heartstrong

Emily has always been a powerhouse of ideas. As the Chief Information Officer (CIO) at a gaming company, her innovative thinking has driven many successful projects. Emily is brilliant, but in the past, she has sometimes struggled to connect emotionally with her team, believing that being right and having the best ideas is enough. Her reputation for being assertive in pushing her concepts was well known.

One day, she noticed that her team's performance was lacking. They weren't delivering their best work, and Emily couldn't understand why. So she gathered her team to introduce a new strategy aimed at streamlining game development. She meticulously crafted the plan, which in her mind was foolproof. However, as she presented the strategy, the team seemed apprehensive and reluctant. Team members exchanged uneasy glances and asked hesitant questions. The more Emily pushed, the more resistance she encountered. Frustration welled up inside her. Why couldn't they see the brilliance of her plan?

After the meeting, during a Tiny Moment of introspection, Emily remembered a recent conversation with a friend who had talked about the importance of emotional intelligence and winning the hearts of those who worked for her. Emily had dismissed the idea at the time, but now, in her moment of frustration, it began to make sense. Being right wasn't enough; the path to win them over would be through their hearts.

Determined to change, Emily adopted a different approach. At the next team meeting, instead of launching straight into her ideas, she began with a simple question: "How are you all doing?" She listened attentively as her team members shared their thoughts and concerns, both personal and professional. For the first time, Emily genuinely engaged with them, showing patience, empathy, and care.

She made it clear that she valued them as individuals and appreciated their ideas. She encouraged questions and embraced suggestions, fostering a collaborative atmosphere. Emily's office, once an intimidating space, became a place for dialogue and creativity. As time passed, she began to understand the importance of creating an environment where everyone felt valued and motivated to contribute.

Gradually the team's dynamic began to shift. The members displayed renewed energy, taking more ownership of projects and showing a level of dedication that had been missing before. The game development strategy, which they had initially met with resistance, was now embraced and improved upon by the team. They were not just following Emily's lead; they were actively shaping the future of the company together.

Emily's journey serves as a powerful reminder that leadership is not just about being right. It's about fostering an environment where everyone feels valued and inspired to contribute to a common goal. Emily's story is a testament to the power of leading with heart, showing that when leaders care genuinely about their people, they can achieve remarkable things together.

CHAPTER TWENTY-SIX

Be Vulnerable

WE OFTEN believe that we must always be the face of unshakable strength, to deny weakness and to "never let them see you sweat." Many people misinterpret vulnerability as weakness.

In battle, this may be true. If your fortress is vulnerable, your enemy may be able to overcome and defeat you. But physical vulnerability is different from emotional vulnerability. Will your personal fortress be opened, exposed, and at risk when you display imperfection, insecurities, or doubts? Perhaps yes, when nefarious people try to use this knowledge against you. But when you're confidently vulnerable, malicious actions against you will be seen for what they are and undermine any success those perpetrators hoped to gain.

Imperfection is real and disarming. It makes people feel better about themselves and more comfortable in personal interactions.

Great leaders understand the power of vulnerability. When you admit your uncertainties, you acknowledge your humanity in a way that connects with others, and those around you will do the same. Something as simple as "I don't know the answer to that" allows others to relax and ask their questions. And it may inspire someone to say, "I know the answer to that."

Vulnerability is not the same as being weak or submissive. On the contrary, it implies the courage to be honest and transparent. It means replacing professional distance with emotional exposure. While we may try to appear perfect, strong, or intelligent in order to gain the respect of others, putting up a pretense can have the opposite effect. Think of how you feel when you perceive someone "putting on a show." Generally we see right through it and feel less connected.

Patrick Lencioni, in his influential book *The Five Dysfunctions of a Team*, emphasizes vulnerability as the cornerstone of trust and the foundation for strong team dynamics. "Team members who are not genuinely open with one another about their mistakes and weaknesses make it impossible to build a foundation for trust," he argues.[1] What great leader doesn't aspire to foster such trust, which serves as the bedrock for the innovation, creativity, and change that leaders should encourage? Lencioni underscores that openness and trust enable teams to embrace risk and collaboration, ultimately driving progress.

Imperfection is real and disarming. It makes people feel better about themselves and more comfortable in personal interactions. It makes a person seem more relatable. For example, occasional mistakes can humanize news anchors, making them more relatable and likable to viewers. These mistakes can display authenticity, humility, and the acknowledgment of one's fallibility, all of which resonate with audiences.

It's the same with great leaders. They acknowledge they aren't perfect. They show their vulnerability. They admit when they make a mistake or don't know something.

As Simon Sinek said, "Great leaders are not the strongest; they are the ones who are honest about their weaknesses. Great leaders are not the smartest; they are the ones who admit how much they don't know. Great leaders can't do everything; they are the ones who look to others to help them. Great leaders don't see themselves as great; they see themselves as human. Great leaders don't try to be perfect; they try to be themselves, and that's what makes them great."[2]

We live in a world of flaws. While portraying "perfection" may work to get people to buy something, it has drawbacks in everyday life, mainly that people have difficulty relating to perfection on a human level. Don't be afraid to be vulnerable by letting people see the real you.

A TINY MOMENT
When You're Wrong, Own It

As we prepared for some office shifts that would have various staff members moving into new spaces, I worked with a team lead to measure the offices affected by the moves. While in the office of someone who would be affected, I said to the team lead, "I assume Barbara knows we're in here." I know how protective people feel about their workspaces, and I always maintain respect for this. Unfortunately, the response to my question was, "I didn't get a chance to talk to her before she went to lunch, but I'm sure it'll be okay."

My response was strong, and I reprimanded the team lead for not making sure Barbara knew we'd be in her space and that we potentially needed to move some things to get proper measurements. It made matters worse that the door was open, and other team members could hear my sharp criticism. The team lead apologized just as Barbara returned from lunch. As it turned out, Barbara had no issue with us being in her office and wasn't surprised because she was aware her office might be affected.

The team lead didn't seem immediately affected by my behavior, but I was. I was also concerned that perhaps she thought she didn't have a right to be hurt because she knew she had made a mistake. I tried to let it go, but I noticed this woman started to build a few walls around herself almost instantly. I began to make excuses, saying that I knew everyone was feeling the strain of the restructuring, but I stopped myself. I took responsibility for my behavior and said I was sorry. She said it was "no big deal" and that she knew she should have checked with Barbara before we went into her office.

I told her that it WAS a big deal. Regardless of what she should have done, there was a more respectful way I could have responded. And I didn't stop there. I asked her if she had witnessed me behaving similarly in the past. I could see her choosing her words carefully, but then she gave me two clear past examples of this behavior. Again, I felt excuses creeping over my tongue with the examples she shared, but I made a point to listen. When she finished, I apologized again, and then I went to three people she had mentioned and acknowledged that my past behavior had perhaps been more hurtful than I realized in the moment.

It takes vulnerability to solicit feedback and apologize for behavior before someone calls you out on it. But doing so creates more open communication. Someone who can create a safe place for vulnerability has the makings of a great leader.

CHAPTER TWENTY-SEVEN

Remember Names

I N MY early thirties, I took the world-famous Dale Carnegie course "How to Win Friends and Influence People." One concept from that course that continues to resonate with me is the idea that a person's name is the sweetest sound to them in any language. Here's an excerpt from the book:

> *Someone says their name, and two seconds later, you don't know it. This is not a memory problem. It is a focus problem.*

> *A person is more interested in his or her own name than in all the other names on earth put together. Remember that name and call it easily and you have paid a subtle and very effective compliment. But forget it or misspell it—and you have placed yourself at a sharp disadvantage. One of the simplest, most obvious and most important ways of gaining goodwill is by remembering names and making people feel important—yet how many of us do it?[1]*

When I heard this, something clicked, and it became one of my bedrock philosophies in life, both professionally and personally. It became woven into my DNA and has always remained at the top of my mind.

How many times have you been embarrassed to chance upon someone whose name you should know but don't? If you're like me, you're embarrassed. It weighs on your mind during the conversation, and you likely try to remember it as the exchange continues, taking your attention away from what the person is saying. If forgetting a person's name can make you feel that uncomfortable, then that's probably a good sign that somewhere in your mind, you know it's important to do better.

Knowing that somebody took the time to remember our names is a simple way to make us feel important.

So many people say, "I am terrible with names, but I never forget a face," as if this were an excuse or permission for them not to bother trying. Everyone can—and should—be good at remembering names by trying and proactively using effective techniques.

The ability to harness the power of using people's names is simply too important to dismiss as "something I am not good at." Not making the effort says to people that they're not worth a little extra effort on your part to make their names stick.

Here are some ways you can improve at remembering names—and it only requires a little more awareness and a modicum of effort:

- First, focus on the person with whom you're having the conversation. If you're distracted and thinking about something else, you have no chance right out of the gate. Take the time to pay attention. A major reason you don't recall names is that you weren't listening. Someone says their name, and two seconds later, you don't know it. This is not a memory problem. It is a focus problem.

- Say their name back to them. Not only does this "sound sweet" to them, but it also forces you to think about the name instead of having it go in one ear and out the other. How often have you heard someone's name only to realize that you immediately forgot it?

- Make associations with the person's name. When I met my friend Dick Rawlings for the first time, I associated him with a baseball glove because Rawlings is a very well-known baseball glove brand. It worked. Every time I saw Dick shortly after meeting him, I would see a big leather glove walking toward me!

- If you do forget, ask! This does not have to be nearly as uncomfortable as it might seem. It is an indication that you care, which people appreciate much more than anything else. Try it with "I'm sorry, I am completely blanking. What's your name again?" You might be surprised how easy it is.

Think of the times you heard someone you deem important use your name and it made you think, "She actually knows my name." Consider how that made you feel and what that said to you about that person. Now, imagine yourself having that impact with everyone you meet. Tiny Moment. Big effect.

A TINY MOMENT
Learning Who's Who

Before I became an agency owner, I had a long and fulfilling career in professional sports. Each day presented me with a myriad of faces, from the head coach to the maintenance crew to the ushers, totaling over one hundred individuals on game nights. The task of remembering names felt quite daunting, especially during my early days in leadership.

Drawing inspiration from Dale Carnegie's timeless wisdom, I was determined to foster meaningful connections with those around me by remembering as many names as possible. In pursuit of this goal, I devised a simple yet effective solution. I printed out the entire employee roster, a document that had the names and titles of everyone associated with the organization. What set it apart was the small photograph next to each person's information.

This roster became my constant companion. I carried it with me wherever I went, and as I crossed paths with more unfamiliar colleagues and staff, I would discreetly reference it, ensuring I could address each person by their name. It was a seemingly small gesture, but its impact was profound. This simple action helped me create a connection with scores of people who were crucial to our organization. The more I used my cheat sheet, the more names I remembered without reference—which, if nothing else, made me feel good about my progress.

Some might argue that I used a shortcut memory aid. However, I would respond by saying I had made the most of the resources at my disposal to create connections with those around me. There was nothing disingenuous or false about the effort I invested in remembering names and acknowledging the importance of every individual.

In the grand fabric of leadership, it's often the tiny, seemingly insignificant gestures that leave the most enduring impressions. My modest use of the employee roster served as a reminder that leadership is not solely about grand acts but also about the small, consistent efforts that foster camaraderie and respect among a team.

CHAPTER TWENTY-EIGHT

Manage Things. Lead People.

THE WORDS "manager" and "leader" are sometimes treated as synonyms. They are not. These two words mean something very different.

Managers pursue prescribed goals. Leaders create vision.

I first became aware of this concept when I read Seth Godin's fabulous book *Tribes*. In the "Leadership Is Not Management" section, Godin describes his view of the difference between the two. It resonated with me then and has stayed with me ever since.

Management promotes stability, maintains systems, exercises authority, and adheres to policies and plans. It is left-brain; it deploys resources to get a known job done. Managers supervise a process they've seen before, striving to make it as fast and cheap as possible. Managers take an established process and endeavor to make it efficient.

Managers have employees and supervise the procedures involved with making stuff. Burger King franchises hire managers.

Leaders, on the other hand, create a vision for creating change. It is a left- and right-brain balance. Leaders expand and develop, initiate new ways to respond better, and aspire to vision and values. Above all, leaders create an environment that cultivates change.

Leaders have followers and inspire them to make change. They focus on finding ways to align and influence those around them. They breed loyalty and dedication.

Both managers and leaders are important for getting things done. But each has their own unique set of functions. While management is unidirectional, leadership is multidirectional.

Managers pursue prescribed goals. Leaders create vision.

Managers are taught or copy things they have seen. Leaders forge new and unique paths.

Managers control risks. Leaders take risks.

Managers exist within known ecosystems. Leaders inspire movements.

Organizations need both managers and leaders to succeed, but the highest-functioning ones develop an environment that does not allow control and regimen to stifle creativity and imagination.

A TINY MOMENT
Reimagine Rather Than Reiterate

An acquaintance of mine owns a car dealership. A few years back, Jim's service department was suffering from poor customer experience and declining business. He knew there were some problems with the operation, but he wasn't exactly sure what they were, much less how to solve them.

What Jim did next demonstrated his understanding of the difference between management and leadership. In the past, he would have talked with his staff about the ways he thought they could better execute the processes they had in place and improve their execution of everyday tasks. But this time, he chose a different path.

Recognizing that genuine leadership requires more than just tweaking existing processes, Jim engaged his team in a collaborative effort to reimagine and innovate the service experience altogether. He initiated a series of open forums with his service team, encouraging them to voice their observations and ideas. Instead of acting like a manager who prescribes solutions, Jim embodied leadership principles by sharing a compelling vision for the service department's future. He wanted to foster an environment of creativity by tapping into the collective imagination and insight of his team to identify the root causes of the problems rather than just focusing on the symptoms.

Jim kicked things off with one single transformational meeting. He started this meeting by emphasizing the importance of providing exceptional customer experiences and making the service center a trusted destination for customers. This vision served as a guiding light for the team and instilled a sense of purpose beyond their routine thinking. Rather than micromanaging operations, Jim empowered his team by steering them away from thinking about how they could execute existing processes more efficiently, and toward "rethinking" their processes altogether, imagining how they might change these processes to adapt to the new competitive environment of higher customer expectations. Jim's leadership style involved fostering a culture of accountability. Instead of imposing strict rules, he encouraged the team to take ownership of the future.

The result was a number of fundamental changes, including a redesign of the physical layout of the service area, the way in which technicians were hired and trained, and even the way in which they scheduled work. These changes sparked a strong turnaround in business. Customer satisfaction increased and revenues followed suit.

Jim's emphasis on empowerment, shared vision, and collaboration not only led to solutions for the identified problems but also transformed the service department into a customer-centric hub within the dealership, all inspired and driven by the collective acumen of his staff. This newfound autonomy empowered them to not only identify and address challenges but also to carry on with improvement in real time, leading to a more agile and responsive service operation moving forward.

As improvements took shape, Jim actively acknowledged and celebrated the efforts of his team. He recognized that positive reinforcement was more effective than rigid performance metrics alone. This approach not only motivated the team but also created a positive and collaborative atmosphere.

Jim's story is a testament to the power of leadership in driving positive change and revitalizing a business.

CHAPTER TWENTY-NINE

Delegate or Bust

"IF YOU want something done right, do it yourself" rarely indicates good leadership. There are moments when it might apply if the experience, knowledge, or skill is so specific that it doesn't make sense to delegate, but for the most part, great leaders help people earn their right to more independence.

An individual without information cannot take responsibility, and in an ideal world, an individual who is given information cannot help but take responsibility.

Delegation is an essential part of my personal style. When doing things, I often ask myself, "How can I never have to do this again?" But with this approach comes great responsibility. You can't delegate and micromanage. You must give up control of what you are handing over. In doing so, you need to share as much information as possible.

An individual without information cannot take responsibility, and in an ideal world, an individual who is given information cannot help but take responsibility.

Delegation indicates trust and optimism, so do so with high expectations. This will motivate your team members to strive for excellence, foster a culture of accountability, and drive overall performance.

In 2017, the *Harvard Business Review* published a Jesse Sostrin article, "To Be a Great Leader, You Have to Learn How to Delegate Well." In determining how to gauge your success at delegation, he posed this question: "If you had to take an unexpected week off work, would your initiatives and priorities advance in your absence?"[1]

Sostrin then outlined four strategies for leaders wanting to improve their delegation skills:

- "Start with your reasons." Beyond sharing the business justification, you need to make people understand why something matters and how they specifically fit into it.

- "Inspire their commitment." Clearly communicating all expectations gives them a solid foundation for delivering a precise outcome or following a particular methodology.

- "Engage at the right level." Clarify from the start what level of engagement will create the right balance of support and accountability.

- "Practice saying 'yes,' 'yes if,' and 'no.'" Say "yes" to requests that will benefit significantly from your insights and skills. Say "yes if" to requests that will benefit from your oversight but not necessarily your involvement. And say "no," combined with an explanation, when your effort and attention are better placed elsewhere.

Delegation is more than a mere distribution of tasks; it is the art of empowerment and the impetus for innovation. By entrusting others with responsibilities, leaders unlock the potential of their teams, fostering collaboration and igniting creativity. The ability to delegate not only lightens the load but also drives organizations toward greatness as it enables leaders to focus on strategy, mentorship, and the bigger picture.

Skilled delegation orchestrates an interplay of trust, skill, and shared purpose. It is a cornerstone skill of effective leadership that transcends tasks and becomes a catalyst for growth and enduring success.

Delegate to Motivate

Benjamin is like a lot of managers I know. A data analyst manager at a telecommunications company, he used to think the best way to get results was to be deeply involved in everything, often doing much of the work himself while his team provided support. After all, given his experience and skills, who else could do a better job than he could?

One evening, he had to miss a family event because he worked late while the rest of his team left at their usual time. Frustrated, Benjamin vented to his wife, saying he should look for a new job. She gently reminded him that maybe it wasn't the job that needed to change.

His wife's insight planted a seed for a Tiny Moment to sprout a few weeks later when Benjamin faced a complex data analysis project. In that moment, he realized this project had the potential to overwhelm him and, inspired by his wife's words, he took a different approach. Instead of tackling the project himself, Benjamin saw an opportunity to empower Jess, a talented data analyst on his team. Recognizing her skills and potential, he asked her to take the lead on the project.

Benjamin sat down with Jess to explain the business reasons behind the analysis and why her expertise made her perfect for the task. He shared all the relevant details, providing context and showing how important the project was to the company's goals. This open conversation ensured that Jess felt a sense of purpose and responsibility.

As Jess dove into the project, Benjamin resisted the urge to micromanage, offering support only when needed. This shift allowed Jess to showcase her abilities, take ownership of the analysis, and bring fresh insights to the table. The project flourished under her leadership, and Benjamin's trust in her capabilities became a catalyst for her professional growth.

Benjamin realized the transformative power of delegation in empowering his team. The project not only met expectations but exceeded them, and Jess's confidence and motivation soared. This Tiny Moment of Benjamin taking a beat to reconsider his approach reinforced the idea that delegation was not just about distributing tasks but also about unlocking the potential within his team.

Inspired by the positive outcome, Benjamin continued to delegate strategically, fostering a culture of collaboration and innovation that elevated the entire telecommunications department to new heights.

CHAPTER THIRTY

Be Transformational

CHANGE. GROW. Innovate.
Expand. Evolve. These words
and concepts embody the spirit
of great leadership.

*Transformational
leaders inspire others
to claim their own
voice and leadership
potential.*

You see, exceptional leadership is
about more than preserving the status
quo; it is about creating change for
good. It is about reaching toward the highest potential of ourselves, those
around us, and the organization.

We all have the potential to grow, gain skills, become more proficient, and
do great things. But this is not an event; it is a long and winding journey.
Motivation, competence, and creativity are drivers for full potential, and
we must activate these attributes to grow.

Potential is a terrible thing to waste, and failing to reach it comes at a
high cost. It cheats the person, the organization, and society at large. It is
our job as leaders to make sure this doesn't happen.

Transformational leaders motivate followers to innovate and embrace
positive change, which in turn helps to grow and shape future success. These
leaders stimulate meaningful change in people and organizational systems
by sharing power, encouraging participation, rallying around purpose, and
creating empowerment.

Transformational leaders inspire others to claim their own voice and leadership potential. They create an environment of change and regularly ask people what they have made better or are doing differently in their jobs. One of the most important callings of leaders is to inspire this change, to expect it, and to celebrate when it comes.

Here's what you might hear from a transformational leader: "This is what I want to accomplish. Here's our goal. How do you think we might want to do this? I had a thought or two, but I'm not sure I'm right."

Transactional leaders, on the other hand, focus on supervision and process. They practice a leadership style that relies on attaining goals through structure, oversight, and a system of rewards and punishments. They determine what and how. Rather than aiming to change or improve the organization, transactional leaders endeavor to reach short-term goals within a framework of company conformity. The rewards or punishments become the "transaction." This results-oriented approach can work well with self-motivated employees, but it is not a good fit for places where creativity and innovative ideas are valued.

Here's what you might hear from a transactional leader: "This is the project. Here's what I want or need you to do. Here's how I want you to do it. When you're done, come back and show me what you've got."

Change and growth are team sports: Everyone must be on board. People who resist will row in the wrong direction and keep the organization from advancing as it can and should. People must embrace expansion and progress to be a part of this (r)evolution. It is through this "transformation" that the company thrives.

An organization that exemplifies this culture needs a transformational leader who understands how to define, personify, and cultivate the environment that nurtures it.

So, what kind of leader do you aspire to be? Transformational or transactional?

A TINY MOMENT
Inspire Free Thinking

It was once said that transformation happens gradually and only through effort every single day. The words of Rahul Sinha add to this thought: "To transform yourself, you don't need to do big things. Just do small things in a big way. Transformation will follow you."

I discovered this at the ad agency when we were developing ideas to promote a healthy living theme for a healthcare client. Unfortunately, the team's first ideas were uninspiring—suggesting the same personality and style we had been using for quite a while. It was time to take a more personal, conversational tone with the writing.

Part of the problem was that the client was not known for out-of-the-box thinking, so the team may have thrown in the towel before they even started. But maybe a bigger issue was that the team had simply become a bit too comfortable with previous approaches and had perhaps slipped into some complacency.

I sent back two rounds of edits with comments but didn't see meaningful improvement. Then, I realized I was trying to manage the process instead of inspiring a different overall perspective.

In thinking about the situation, it occurred to me that a common creative error is being too broad in an effort to appeal to everyone. This can sometimes result in reaching no one because the messaging lacks personalization. I held a small brainstorming meeting and encouraged a group discussion about this issue. We asked one tiny question, which led to one big transformational conversation.

The group discussion led to the idea of writing with a selection of personas in mind instead of a mass audience. Recognizing that positive change can emerge from subtle shifts, we began to personalize our content, tailoring it to specific individuals within our target demographic. This shift resulted in measurable success, as our articles resonated more deeply with our audience, leading to increased engagement and positive feedback.

The small change in how I asked the team for the revisions inspired a completely fresh approach with a series of specialized articles. "Healthy eating" became "The benefits of macrobiotics." "The importance of exercise" became "How a fifteen-minute walk at lunch will change your life."

By taking a moment to remind and encourage my team to think freely, I led them toward better results. Transformation does not happen when thinking is transactional and prescribed. It happens when it is unencumbered and inspired. Most often, the key is not to give them the answer but to guide them to discover it themselves.

CHAPTER THIRTY-ONE

Be Gray

GET A lot of quizzical faces from aspiring leaders when I suggest they "be gray." It certainly isn't a term commonly used to recommend leadership behavior. The skies might be gray, and hair might be gray, but to think of that word as a positive human disposition might seem odd.

Let me explain.

Being gray in leadership means refraining from giving a clear and decisive answer when asked a question. Thinking gray can often be an unusual behavior for leaders. We think of leaders as great captains who are bold and decisive people strongly influenced by their passions and prejudices. Can you imagine Steve Jobs or Elon Musk thinking gray?

Here's the thing: If you are the one who provides the definitive answer to every question your team asks, you condition people to expect that they don't have to think. And sometimes, that's what they want. The leader runs the show, and if something is to be done, people want to know what that leader's opinion is so they can make them happy. It's easy and safe. You can't get mad at people for doing what you told them to do.

If you are the one who provides the definitive answer to every question your team asks, you condition people to expect that they don't have to think.

However, this is hardly a transformational scenario in which people freely think, openly participate, and confidently act with empowerment. It does not represent an environment that acknowledges that taking initiative (including small failures along the way) is necessary to grow, gain confidence, and achieve full potential.

In the previous chapter, when we talked about the value of being a transformational leader, we touched upon some cultural aspects of transformative environments. We mentioned that in such a setting, you will likely hear the leader(s) say something like, "I had a thought or two, but I'm not sure I'm right."

Now, you wouldn't use this approach for all questions. For example, you wouldn't use this approach when someone asks you what you want for lunch. Being gray is reserved for situations that have various options for groups to envision and examine before selecting the best option to pursue.

According to Steven Sample, the former president of the University of Southern California and author of *The Contrarian's Guide to Leadership*, the "essence of thinking gray is this: don't form an opinion about an important matter until you've heard all the relevant facts and arguments, or until circumstances force you to form an opinion without recourse to all the facts."[1]

However, many top political and military leaders have used a gray "wait-and-see" approach. George Washington, Winston Churchill, and Martin Luther King Jr. knew the value of suspending judgment about important matters, especially when dealing with incoming intelligence, until the last possible moment.

One of the most beneficial results of applying a gray presence is the confidence gained by the team along the way. Many studies show that the mind becomes much sharper at a mental or physical activity after you do it many times. That's what will happen with your team. The more they respond to your gray approach by thinking, synthesizing, and concluding, the more proficient they will become at it.

F. Scott Fitzgerald once described the real test of a first-rate mind as the ability to hold two opposing thoughts at the same time while still retaining the ability to function.

So, the next time someone asks you, "What do you think?," respond by being gray and saying something like, "I have some initial thoughts based on the information given, but first, I'd love to hear what you think."

A TINY MOMENT
Empower People to Think Before They Ask

When employees move to a company with good leaders, there's often an adjustment period where they must find their way as decision-makers. Bill was an extreme example of this.

Bill joined us as an office manager reporting to Jean in HR. Jean was thrilled when he came on board because, previously, so much of his work had been part of her responsibility. She quickly learned, though, that Bill's presence wasn't reducing her workload because he came to her with everything. "What size Post-its should I order?" "Where do you want the water bottles?" "For the team social, should I order IPAs or domestics?"

She answered all of his questions because she had the experience to know, and it felt easier to do it than inspire him to think for himself.

One day, she actually had some breathing room, which allowed her to think about it differently. When Bill came to her again asking for advice on where to put a new printer for the creative team, she started to take control of the answer but instead asked, "I'm not sure. What are your thoughts?"

She saw in Bill's reaction that he wasn't used to having an opinion. He was used to being told what to do. He stammered for a bit and then offered a suggestion. She knew it wasn't going to work in his suggested location because people were more likely to run into the printer than use it, but she let him talk through it until he realized for himself the mistake. When he tried to use that as an out and put it back on Jean to decide, she didn't take the bait. "Why don't you look around and think about it? I'll meet you later this afternoon to hear your suggestions," she said.

That afternoon, he presented her with three options, one of which never would have occurred to her but made the most sense. She told him as much, and she saw the pride on his face. After that, he came to her less frequently, and when he did, he usually had a suggestion in his pocket. One day, most of the general questions just stopped.

We as leaders have countless opportunities to be gray, and we make progress with someone's professional growth every time we are. It's interesting to watch the evolution of team members from the Tiny Moment you are gray with them for the first time until they start to get it and as a result, become far better prepared for interactions in the future.

CHAPTER THIRTY-TWO

Who's Got the Monkey?

CERTAIN BOOKS and articles truly make a mark on you. I have a Hall of Fame for the ones that have had the biggest impact on me. One memorable inductee into my Hall is a *Harvard Business Review* article I read many years ago. It had a profoundly powerful effect at that stage in my leadership life.

> By accepting the monkey, the leader has voluntarily assumed a position subordinate to their subordinate.

"Who's Got the Monkey?" was originally published in 1974 and it remains as applicable today as it was then.[1] In it, William Oncken and Donald Wass describe the "monkey-on-the-back" syndrome that occurs when the leader consciously takes over the work that the subordinate should do. Oncken and Wass interpret this as a combination of "self-imposed" and "subordinate-imposed" time.

A monkey-on-the-back incident can happen anywhere at any time. Oncken and Wass provide an example: In a passing moment in a hallway, a leader comes across a team member who mentions a problem they are having. When the team member asks the leader for their thoughts and opinions, the leader pauses. They know enough to get involved but not enough to make the on-the-spot decision expected of them. That's the fateful moment the leader takes the monkey from the team member, saying, "I'm glad you brought this up. Let me think about it and I'll let you know."

By accepting the monkey, the leader has voluntarily assumed a position subordinate to their subordinate.

In a commentary on the article written many years after the original publication, leadership guru Stephen Covey says that while business practices and cultures have changed since 1974, command and control stubbornly remain a common practice. "Management thinkers and executives have discovered in the last decade that bosses cannot just give a monkey back to their subordinates and then go merrily along their way," said Covey. "Empowering subordinates is hard and complicated work."[2] It depends on a trusting relationship between a leader and their team.

When you think about it, isn't that the goal of this book? All the thoughts and ideas in it are dedicated to creating a world filled with capable people you share with, trust, and respect. Do this and you won't struggle with command and control. There will be trust between you and your people and, as a result, there will be fewer monkeys on the loose in the first place.

A TINY MOMENT
It's Better to Give Than to Receive

Walking through the hallway, Amanda was deep in thought about the upcoming client presentation when James, one of her dedicated team members, approached her.

"We've been working on those projects for the Maxwell account, and I need your input on how to prioritize them. I'm not sure which ones should be at the top of the list," James said. "Can you take a look at it and let me know what you think?"

Amanda started to agree to James's request. After all, she wanted to be a good leader and help a team member. But then, in one Tiny Moment, she realized that if she took on James's request, she'd pile more work onto her already full plate. As a result, her work and the overall success of the team would suffer. In this moment of inspiration, rather than taking on the task, she suggested James take the first crack at the project.

"I trust your judgment," Amanda said. "Lay out what you think is the best order based on the client's objectives and timelines. Then, bring it to me for review, and we can fine-tune it together. This way, you'll get more practice making these decisions, and we'll both make the most of our time."

When James submitted his prioritized list, Amanda reviewed it, offering constructive feedback and making a few adjustments. Together, they finalized the project order, ensuring they had prioritized the critical tasks.

By encouraging James to take the lead, Amanda not only reinforced her trust in his abilities but also avoided the common leadership pitfall of taking on someone else's work. This approach empowered James and freed Amanda to focus on other strategic tasks, ultimately benefiting the entire team.

Amanda's experience really stuck with me. She showed me that great leadership isn't about doing everything yourself but about guiding your team to handle challenges on their own. It is a powerful reminder that sometimes, the best way to lead is to step back and let others step up.

CHAPTER THIRTY-THREE

Stay Balanced Between Being and Doing

WE ALL love the doers in our organizations. They are action-oriented problem-solvers who become proactive and assertive when things need to get done. After all, our business strategies, plans, and initiatives require effective execution to be successful. Yet despite how essential the "Doing" is, leadership must deliver on something well above and beyond it—the "Being."

The danger comes when we carry this mindset into our leadership role, believing that by working longer, harder, and smarter than our team, we'll automatically inspire by example.

The concept of Being vs. Doing as a leader has its roots in the practice of mindful leadership, which focuses on the conscious cultivation of Being present, open-minded, and compassionate when interacting with team members. According to Michael Carroll, author of *The Mindful Leader*, "mindfulness is our natural ability to be fully present in our life—alert, open and engaged."[1]

If leaders are not awake in this way, they relinquish the capacity to understand what is going on with their employees, what is holding them back from being great, and what they can do to help them achieve more. Being is a deeper, more aware layer of leadership that involves investing time in seeking out open communication, building personal connections, and inspiring through compassion and vision.

The Being component of leadership is far more important than the Doing component, although the Doing part is also important. After all, leaders often must buckle down and get things done themselves, especially when their skills, experience, and position make them the most appropriate, even necessary, person to execute on a particular project or task. However, a leader's presence with their team has a more significant impact on the overall culture of the organization than how they perform in terms of Doing.

Sometimes, the Doing side can seem easier ("I'll just do it myself") and can bring quick results. But the Being side is how you apply the concepts and techniques in this book. It is in Being that you can work with people to make them better and to understand how they go about their work so you can help them become more proficient and productive.

People need mentorship, guidance, and training to grow and become their best. And this simply doesn't happen when a leader's time is dominated by Doing at the expense of spending quality time just Being with people.

As we build our professional careers, our skills as individual contributors quite often mark our accomplishments. We add value by getting things done. We're efficient and quality Doers. The danger comes when we carry this mindset into our leadership role, believing that by working longer, harder, and smarter than our team, we'll automatically inspire by example. Success as a leader depends on delivering value to the organization in a different way. We need to do less and lead more to influence others effectively. This softer skill set of authentic leadership—the ability to work with and through others—is regrettably in scarce supply.

The Being side can be less visible and requires that you spend time going deeper to do some essential interior work. It requires making a conscious effort to tap into empathy, interpersonal perspective, and win-win partnering. There are way more leaders who drive execution by action alone and far fewer who can do that while fully holding and occupying the Being space. You inspire those around you by Being engaged in conversation and action. Sometimes, this requires putting away the to-do list and focusing on leading through connecting, listening, and conferring.

As Pam Hernandez, founder and CEO of The Right Reflection, says, "Leadership is as much about who you are as what you do."[2] Use this as inspiration as you strive to utilize Being to be the great leader you are and save the Doing for when what you do is truly indispensable.

A TINY MOMENT

Know When to Leave Doing to Others

In her role as vice president of a busy marketing firm, McKenna shouldered increasing leadership responsibilities while managing some of the organization's most significant clients. These clients played a pivotal role in fueling the agency's growth, intensifying McKenna's sense of responsibility for the relationships. She found herself acting as a "doer-in-chief," deeply immersed in day-to-day client work beyond her official title.

Falling into the trap of "If you want something done, do it yourself," McKenna realized the approach's lack of scalability. Despite her proficiency in executing projects, she grappled with the challenge of transitioning from working on tasks to working with people. The need arose to delegate responsibilities and grow her people professionally, which required her to entrust tasks to others, even when she could proficiently execute them herself.

McKenna needed to make the shift from working IN the company to working ON the company. She needed to delegate responsibilities that she would typically do herself. While she knew she could proficiently execute these tasks with little difficulty, she could not always say the same for her staff.

The turning point arrived when McKenna faced a project from an important client that exceeded her bandwidth. Recognizing the necessity to delegate, she invested time and energy to bring a team member up to speed by reviewing how the project would be approached, possible solutions to various issues, pitfalls to watch for and in general—all valuable advice for how to proceed.

This experience, born out of necessity, evolved into a Tiny Moment—a revelation for McKenna. She did not find it easy to assign challenging projects to others, but there was a simplicity in that moment that created the clarity needed to redefine her role. To be the transformational leader she wanted to be, she needed to continue her own professional growth in order to stimulate the growth of others. The development of people is the highest calling of leadership, and doing so often requires the leader to shift from a Doing to a Being mindset.

This situation propelled McKenna to shift her focus from task-oriented work to a more global role within the company. As she steered others toward specific tasks, she assumed a leadership role that allowed her to see the bigger organizational picture. It became clear that being present for the team dedicated to the work was more powerful than doing the work herself. McKenna's epiphany marked the beginning of her journey into becoming the transformational leader the company needed.

CHAPTER THIRTY-FOUR

Encourage and Teach Critical Thinking

C RITICAL THINKING is an essential skill that allows individuals to gather data, develop insights, and draw conclusions to make informed decisions. When teams employ critical thinking, they gain enhanced problem-solving abilities to arrive at objective and astute conclusions. It

Few skills yield greater results in an organization than using sound critical thinking across the board.

is essential in both professional and personal settings as we navigate the complexities of the modern world.

Critical thinking empowers individuals to form their own opinions and make decisions based on evidence and reason rather than unquestioningly accepting the ideas of others. It enhances workplace skills such as creativity, analytical competency, communication, and emotional intelligence. It involves analyzing information, identifying patterns, and evaluating evidence, skills essential for effective problem-solving in any domain.

Critical thinkers approach problems from different angles and consider alternative solutions. Ultimately, it makes it easier to evaluate the strengths and weaknesses of various options to arrive at the best possible solution.

Unfortunately, employees are generally not delivered to our doorstep ready to think critically. Like any other skill, critical thinking can take some tutoring, practice, and experience to cultivate. Teaching critical thinking is a central responsibility of leaders. Few skills yield greater results in an organization than using sound critical thinking across the board.

To teach and foster critical thinking among your team members:

- Ask open-ended questions that require them to analyze and evaluate information. This will help develop the habit of questioning assumptions and considering alternative mindsets.

- Offer hints of diverse perspectives and encourage the consideration of different viewpoints.

- Teach strategies for solving problems, such as breaking complex problems down into smaller parts and making connections between ideas.

- Encourage them to reflect on their thought processes to enhance awareness of their biases and assumptions.

"Why?" and "What if?" are the cornerstones of critical thinking, and by offering these questions to those around you, you invite them to think and be heard in new ways. Most people want to exercise their minds, and many are surprised to find what they're capable of, especially when part of a brainstorming team. Teaching and building these skills allow us to grow the company because more projects can be taken on when there is greater solution-oriented brainpower at work.

As my career evolved, I increasingly became a strategic elder. I've been at this a long time and have a certain level of success, which indicates that I am a clear and critical thinker. But that's not enough. I must offer others the opportunity to join the discussion and practice critical thinking through personal and group discussions, impromptu debates, and project management. Spark curiosity by sharing your business rationale behind certain thoughts and ideas.

Teaching critical thinking is a valuable investment in the organization's future success. By promoting independent thinking, problem-solving, creativity, and effective communication, employees will develop the skills necessary to succeed in our modern world.

A TINY MOMENT
Question Everything

Early in my leadership career, I took the concept of critical thinking to heart and initiated a subtle yet transformative shift in my daily interactions. I understood that critical thinking was not just a personal skill but a force that could enhance the culture of the workplace. Armed with the belief that fostering critical thinking could elevate the problem-solving abilities of my team, I began to implement small changes in my approach.

Instead of conventional directives, I started incorporating open-ended questions into my conversations with team members. These small, in-the-moment questions encouraged analysis and evaluation, prompting my colleagues to delve deeper into their thought processes. In one Tiny Moment, I spontaneously introduced an impromptu group discussion (I'm not afraid to call it a debate) about two different approaches we could take with a client project. At that moment, I wanted to create space for diverse perspectives to emerge. By doing so, I not only cultivated an environment that valued critical thinking but also gave my team the opportunity to exercise their minds collaboratively. This shift, although subtle, soon rippled through the rest of the agency as individuals noticed me questioning more assumptions, considering alternative viewpoints, and approaching problems with a broader mindset.

Eventually, my commitment to exemplifying and teaching critical thinking extended to more formal departmental strategic training sessions. I actively shared the business rationale behind certain decisions, often in small extemporaneous conversations, sparking curiosity and encouraging others to contribute to the ongoing discussions. This collaborative approach enriched the team's collective intelligence and fueled a sense of empowerment and ownership. The result was a workplace where employees were not just workers but also critical thinkers equipped with the skills to navigate the complexities of the modern world.

The impact of my shift in behavior, essentially driven by a focus on asking questions, became evident as projects gained a new level of solution-oriented brainpower. My organization thrived as independent thinking, creativity, and effective communication became second nature. My dedication to critical thinking proved to be a valuable investment, not only in the professional development of individuals but also in future success.

CHAPTER THIRTY-FIVE

Be a Lifelong Learner

OUR WORLD is continuously evolving, with technology, ingenuity, and know-how advancing rapidly. You need more than what you know today to be successful in the future. You can milk your current skill set and knowledge base for a while without growing, but eventually, you'll fall behind and become a pretender.

A lifelong learning mindset embraces challenges, change, and critique as a path to continual growth.

In her weekly newsletter, psychologist Gemma Leigh Roberts, PhD, said the half-life of a skill is about five years.[1] The term "half-life," as used in this context, refers to the time it takes for a skill to become half as valuable as it was before. Therefore, according to Dr. Roberts, much of what you learned ten years ago is now obsolete and half of what you learned five years ago is irrelevant. If you work for fifty years, think of all the new skills and knowledge you need to stay relevant in your job!

Lifelong learning is gaining knowledge and new skills beyond formal education and throughout life. This involves studying new topics and developing an open-minded, positive attitude about the dynamic nature of the world. A curious and growth-oriented mindset creates future possibilities, both professionally and personally.

A lifelong learning mindset embraces challenges, change, and critique as a path to continual growth. Accept that skill acquisition requires effort, improvement is possible, and obstacles are not a reason to stop your progress. Look for opportunities to expand your knowledge and understanding. Probe and push with a curiosity that borders on skepticism, resolutely seeking answers to your questions. Have a thirst that never gets fully quenched.

Good leaders constantly read, learn, practice, rehearse, assess, change, and evolve. They consult and converse with other leaders. They remain open to the world and treat everything and everyone as an opportunity to learn.

In his undelivered Nov. 22, 1963, speech, President John F. Kennedy acknowledged the importance of continually developing knowledge, writing, "Leadership and learning are indispensable to each other."

Lifelong learning does not have to be complicated. Sure, it involves reading and a workshop or webinar here and there, but at its simplest level, learning is about being curious. Ask questions, listen carefully, and then ask more questions. Have you noticed how engaged people become when you ask them about something they are knowledgeable about?

There is nothing in this world you can't learn by asking someone if you're willing to shut up, listen, and focus on the answer. Remember:

- Be curious . . . about everything. Curiosity may have killed the cat, but it sustains a lifelong learner.

- Everyone can teach you something.

- Have diverse interests and passions.

- Never be afraid to leave your comfort zone.

- Don't be afraid to ask about things you don't know about. Get comfortable with being uncomfortable.

- Be open to different perspectives than your own.

A TINY MOMENT
A Lesson in Learning

Bruce has been at his job for several years, finding comfort and camaraderie in his daily routine. He loves his coworkers and feels no rush to climb the corporate ladder. He is content to enjoy his steady success and not seek a leadership role.

But contentment can be deceptive. It can create a false sense of security. A while back, Bruce started noticing shifts in the industry. Technology was simplifying tasks that had once been his responsibility. When he talked about these changes with his colleagues, they shrugged them off, believing any real impact was still far off.

Despite their complacency, Bruce made a small personal change. On his commute each morning, he began listening to a podcast about the future of his industry. When he found something particularly intriguing, he would read more about it in his spare time. One day, his supervisor caught him watching a video on AI, which led to a long conversation about what Bruce had been learning. His boss was impressed by Bruce's curiosity and enthusiasm for the future.

As time passed, the once-distant technology became a present reality. Bruce's department had to be streamlined, with fewer people needed to manage the work. While others rolled their eyes at the advances that led to job cuts, Bruce s proactive learning secured his place.

His company didn't give Bruce an official leadership title, but his colleagues started to see him differently. Leadership isn't always about having a fancy title or overseeing others. Sometimes, it's about how you approach your work and career, making continuous learning a passion and staying ahead of industry trends. This is what true leaders do.

For Bruce, the Tiny Moment came when he decided to respond to the technological changes impacting his job. In that moment, he chose to acknowledge that the future is always closer than we think and to keep pace with the advancements shaping his field. This decision, driven by personal curiosity and a desire to stay relevant, marks him as a leader in the eyes of those around him.

CHAPTER THIRTY-SIX

Manage by Walking Around

MANAGEMENT BY Walking Around (MBWA) is a management style in which a leader involves themselves in the daily operations of the workplace by visiting employees, observing work processes, and communicatinG in person with staff. The

> *"A body can pretend to care, but they can't pretend to be there."*
>
> *—Texas Bix Bender*

goal of this close-up interaction is to better understand employee performance, needs, and feedback. The MBWA approach prioritizes interpersonal relationships and a high-touch style in contrast to an over-concentration on task completion.

The concept of MBWA originated with HP's David Packard in the 1940s and was popularized by business guru and best-selling author Tom Peters in his book *In Search of Excellence*.

According to Peters, the first time he and his colleague observed MBWA, "We were just enchanted by it. . . . I am really in love with it as more or less a metaphor for being in touch . . . the discipline of getting out of your office and getting close to where the work is really done."[1] One of Peters's often used phrases to describe MBWA, quoted from Texas Bix Bender, is "A body can pretend to care, but they can't pretend to be there."[2] The implementation of MBWA has become popular among organizations as a method of enhancing communication and shaping a more engaged workforce. By establishing strong relationships with employees and gaining a personal eyewitness understanding of their work environment, leaders can identify problems as they unfold and spot positives to highlight and celebrate.

Keeping your finger on the pulse of an organization or team cannot be done from a distance. It requires hands-on availability and visibility. By walking around and observing employees in their work environment, leaders can gain insights into the challenges their people face, identify areas for improvement, and provide feedback and guidance.

Team chemistry requires orchestration, and as the conductor of that orchestra, you need to be visible. Someone struggling with a challenge might feel trapped at their desk as they try to work through it. Finding the courage and appropriate time to step away and seek assistance can be a daunting proposition for them, especially if they have no idea of their leader's availability or approachability. But if a leader is walking through the room with an obvious willingness to engage, listen, and help, issues can get resolved before they fester into bigger problems.

Regularly walking around and engaging with employees creates an environment that encourages open communication, enabling workers to share their thoughts, ideas, and concerns comfortably. This type of interaction can stimulate innovation, problem-solving, and a more positive workplace culture. By interacting with employees on a regular basis, leaders can identify areas where employees may need additional training or support to improve their performance and advance their careers.

The application of MBWA is more challenging than ever in our virtual work-from-anywhere world, in which a physical space to walk around is less available. This means two things. First, we must make the most of the facetime we do have while we are working together. Second, we must learn how to reach people's hearts and minds without being physically there all the time.

As a Wharton study asserts, "A physical-to-virtual translation of MBWA can be implemented, but it requires a new way of planning and prioritizing how we execute through our day."[3] In other words, since you can't always just get up and spontaneously interact, MBWA may require more planning and purposefulness. However, while the workplace may be virtual, the essence of MBWA is still the same. It requires pushing away from work in front of you and listening to what is going on with your people as they toil in the trenches.

Remember that great leaders stay far enough ahead of their people to lead, but close enough to understand and relate to them. Take the time to see and be seen and to hear and be heard.

A TINY MOMENT

You Don't Need to Be There to "Be There"

When a real estate firm elevated my friend Lynn to team lead for a group of agents, she followed in the footsteps of her previous supervisor by offering an "open door" policy for those reporting to her. But a few weeks into her new job, she realized that no one had approached her door, and she had only learned of challenges when attending scheduled meetings or when problems had reached the point of needing her involvement. When she asked why agents hadn't brought the problems to her earlier, they said, "Your door is open, but you always looked busy. We didn't want to add to your plate."

When Lynn returned to her office, she realized how distant she was from the pulse of daily operations. She was busy, but a lot of what she was busy with was her own incoming data and ideas, not with the fires that could have possibly been avoided if she'd been aware they were simply smoldering.

Lynn knew she needed to adjust and she made a commitment right then and there. In that Tiny Moment of realization, she committed to making a conscious effort to stroll through the open workspace, engaging with her team, observing their processes, and actively listening to their concerns. She stuck an "MBWA" Post-it to her monitor to remind herself to manage by walking around.

This adjustment in Lynn's approach quickly bore fruit. Barriers that had existed between management and employees began to dissolve. Her presence became a symbol of accessibility and approachability. As she walked around, she not only identified potential bottlenecks in projects but also discovered hidden talents and innovative solutions among her team members. The personal touch of MBWA allowed her to address challenges before they escalated, creating a more collaborative and positive work environment.

When the virtual work-from-anywhere landscape arrived, it presented its challenges to Lynn's MBWA effort, but Lynn, undeterred, embraced the shift. She maintained a consistent presence, ensuring that her team felt supported and connected. By purposefully planning her interactions, she continued to foster open communication, sparking creativity and problem-solving discussions. In the end, her commitment to being present, even in a virtual setting, demonstrated that the essence of MBWA lies not just in physical proximity, but in the leader's dedication to understanding and uplifting their team.

CHAPTER THIRTY-SEVEN

Trust but Verify

UNFORTUNATELY, THERE is more to delegating than giving someone a task. After identifying a capable person for the assignment, you must take the time to help them understand how to be successful. Then, you must stay close enough to the situation to ensure they

You don't need to hover and micromanage to ensure positive results.

succeed. While you feel you have the right person with the right skill set and enough experience for the assignment, you simply cannot know how they will do until they get started and make progress.

A "dump and run" won't work here. You must check in periodically, more often in the early stages, then steadily pull back as you gain more confidence that things are going well.

"Trust but verify" is a Russian proverb widely associated with Ronald Reagan. Although he did not originate the expression, he certainly brought it into the modern lexicon when he used it on several occasions in the 1980s to characterize nuclear disarmament discussions with the Soviet Union. Reagan used it to emphasize the verification procedures enabling both sides to monitor compliance.

A study by Claus Langfred, a professor of organizational behavior at George Mason University, found that too much trust can depress performance.[1] He found that excessive trust leads to less monitoring and a relatively low awareness of activities, negatively affecting performance through poor process, coordination, and support. Deliberate monitoring is important, regardless of the level of trust. A little healthy skepticism never hurt anyone or any team.

As a leader, you know that the only way for your people to grow is to give them more and more runway to work on projects independently. However, you also know they need and want collaboration. No one likes working in a vacuum. They want a certain amount of interaction with those around them to validate their work and get advice and ideas that may help them and build their confidence as they move forward. This is exactly what "trust but verify" means.

The stakes are too high in business to assume everyone will do things well. But you don't need to hover and micromanage to ensure positive results. Adopt the right level of monitoring for the person and situation. Even if you must play a larger role early on, look for opportunities to pull back over time. If you have the right person and things go well, ultimately, you will have the confidence to distance yourself and "verify" only every so often, perhaps within the context of your standard reporting processes.

Don't buy the adage, "Hire good people and get out of their way." If you do, they often find their own things to get in their way. This is not meant to demean them; it just means they're human, and they may not be ready to run solo.

A TINY MOMENT
Find the Appropriate Balance

Shortly after I promoted Jean to the position of director of game operations at the professional hockey organization where I worked, she received an urgent call from a supplier reporting a potential issue with a shipment of supplies. As Jean investigated the matter, she realized that there had been miscommunication within her team about specific delivery instructions. The mistake, though minor, had the potential to escalate into a real problem.

Jean identified Rose as the team member responsible for the oversight. But instead of reprimanding her immediately, Jean decided to approach the situation differently. She invited Rose for a one-on-one meeting and included a discussion of the incident, asking open-ended questions to understand Rose's thought process and the challenges she faced. It became evident that Rose had misunderstood a critical aspect of the client's requirements.

In that moment, Jean recognized the importance of both trusting her team and verifying key details. She realized that while Rose was highly capable, misinterpretations could still occur. From then on, Jean integrated regular check-ins into her leadership style, not as a means of micromanaging, but as a way to enhance communication and avoid potential misunderstandings. This Tiny Moment became a catalyst for Jean's growth as a leader, reinforcing the idea that deliberate monitoring was a valuable aspect of trust, ensuring the success of her team and the satisfaction of their clients.

This Tiny Moment of empathetic leadership and collaborative problem-solving shifted Jean's understanding, prompting her to adopt a nuanced approach to "trust but verify."

CHAPTER THIRTY-EIGHT

Enforce Accountability

MY AD agency reserves our company's core values for our most cherished principles. They are the essential codes of our conduct, like creativity, agility, and strategy.

Among the most central of these core values is accountability. Acting with accountability is so paramount to how we work that we could not operate without

"Look at the word responsibility— 'response-ability'— the ability to choose your response."

—Stephen Covey

it. It holds a place on the Mount Rushmore of our core values. It is a fundamental backbone of our organization, governing how we work and influencing how we support each other every day.

At the heart of accountability is taking responsibility for our actions, decisions, and behavior. This means owning up to the good and the bad outcomes of our choices. Assuming accountability requires accepting responsibility for our choices and actions by setting attainable goals, taking steps to achieve them, and keeping track of our progress. When leaders cultivate a culture of accountability within a workplace, it enhances efficiency, raises team spirit, and encourages a sense of commitment and responsibility toward the organization's objectives.

Here's what Stephen Covey says about accountability's roots in responsibility: "Look at the word responsibility—'response-ability'—the ability to choose your response. Highly proactive people recognize that responsibility. They do not blame circumstances or conditions for their behavior. Accountable behavior is the product of their own conscious choice, based on personal values."[1]

Real accountability happens in a culture that supports trust and genuine teamwork. It comes with an honesty that acknowledges where things can improve and a humility to look in the mirror and be honest with ourselves when things go wrong. We must overcome our resistance to calling ourselves out on our personal performance and choices. When we avoid holding ourselves accountable, we grossly downplay the importance of following through. "Do what you say and say what you do" is an ethic that requires following up on the commitment made upon accepting an assignment and establishing a completion date.

The absence of accountability can stem from a workplace or team environment that tolerates subpar performance. Alternatively, it can result from individuals who consistently fall short of expectations. If leaders don't address these negative patterns, they can muddle the clarity of roles and responsibilities and further undermine accountability. With repeated occurrences, we may convince ourselves that failing to follow through on our commitments holds no real significance. This kind of avoidance and denial can severely damage our capacity to uphold trust with others and maintain confidence in ourselves.

From a broader context, accountability weakens or falls apart altogether if a business operates with fuzzy priorities or vague expectations. When priorities and expectations are clearly defined, employees can align their actions with the company's goals and objectives. This alignment fosters a sense of ownership and responsibility among team members, further strengthening the accountability culture. However, this sense of ownership and responsibility can quickly dissipate when a business operates without these clear definitions.

When employees are unsure of what an organization expects of them, they may become demotivated, leading to a lack of accountability. In this scenario, individuals may not take responsibility for their actions or feel a sense of ownership in achieving the company's goals, resulting in missed deadlines, poor-quality work, and a decrease in overall productivity. When individuals are not held accountable for their actions, it creates an environment of mistrust and resentment. This can make it difficult for team members to work together effectively, further eroding the company's overall performance.

Ultimately, a lack of accountability leads to a breakdown in communication and collaboration within a team.

Consultant Karim Bashay illustrates this point in *HR* magazine: "Expectations that aren't communicated can grind progress to a halt. Not only do these implicit expectations result in confusion over tasks, but they also cause tension in relationships."[2] Ultimately, this then leads to an organization plagued by distrust.

There is no denying that accountability demands considerable effort and dedication from both leaders and team members. It is not always easy and requires a certain level of commitment, honesty, and transparency. Acknowledging mistakes or taking ownership of undesired results can be challenging, but it is essential for running a successful organization.

Without accountability, a company will struggle to achieve its goals and objectives, leading to a decline in overall performance. It is imperative to establish a culture of accountability and strive to maintain it through consistent effort and dedication.

A TINY MOMENT
Choose to Own It

Bobby, a meticulous economics research analyst, found himself in a culture that emphasized the indispensable principle of accountability. As he went about his workday, he began to realize that small shifts in behavior could significantly impact the dynamics of his team and the overall success of the organization. The pivotal moment for Bobby occurred during a team meeting when his manager—in response to some recent situations—took time to re-emphasize the importance of not only meeting deadlines but also taking ownership of the outcomes, both good and bad.

This Tiny Moment of admonition resonated with Bobby and sparked a renewed perspective of accountability. He realized that accountability is more than an abstract concept; it is a conscious choice rooted in personal values. It became clear that true accountability demanded proactive choices, a commitment to taking responsibility, and a refusal to blame external circumstances for one's actions. This realization prompted him to set more attainable goals, track his progress diligently, and, most importantly, foster a culture of trust and teamwork within his research team.

Bobby's newfound commitment to accountability manifested in tangible ways. He took the initiative to communicate clear expectations with his team members, ensuring everyone understood their roles and responsibilities. By embracing a proactive approach and aligning individual actions with the team's overarching goals, Bobby witnessed a boost in his efficiency and team orientation.

In the broader context of the company, Bobby's dedication to accountability became a catalyst for positive change in others. As he emphasized the importance of clarity in his priorities and expectations, he inspired those around him to adopt a renewed sense of ownership and responsibility as well, creating a domino effect that strengthened communication, collaboration, and performance.

CHAPTER THIRTY-NINE

Personify the Heart of a Servant

EFFECTIVE LEADERS do not view themselves as superior or wear their title like a medal. Instead, they guide, mentor, and lead by helping others. The philosophy that the leader should serve the greater good is the basis for the servant leadership style.

For a servant-leader, the team and the organization are the top priority. The focus is always on helping others excel as much as possible. This means putting aside personal objectives and making sacrifices. When a leader is completely devoted to their team, the company becomes more successful, benefiting everyone involved. A leader's everyday persona should be that of a servant.

The leader serves people so that they can, in turn, better serve the organization and eventually become servant-leaders themselves.

According to several historical accounts, the earliest recorded reference to leaders playing the role of servant comes from the 1700s when the autocratic but enlightened King Frederick II of Prussia portrayed himself as "the first servant of the state." Robert K. Greenleaf later coined the phrase "servant-leadership" in a 1970 essay and put it into organizational use while working as an executive at AT&T. Greenleaf described a servant-leader as one who shares power and puts the needs of the employees first.[1]

Greenleaf professed that the leader's highest calling is to "serve the people," helping them to grow, become more capable, and achieve greater autonomy. His perspective was that a leader should be someone workers can relate to. Servant-leaders ask questions such as:

- "What can I do for you?"

- "What resources do you need to utilize your talents?"

- "Are there any impediments in your way?"

With this perspective, the leader serves people so that they can, in turn, better serve the organization and eventually become servant-leaders themselves. In this respect, the leader is at the bottom of the totem pole. What a concept!

Imagine yourself being an orchestra conductor, as described by Itay Talgam in a powerful TED Talk.[2] After a decade-long conducting career in his native Israel, Talgam reinvented himself as a "conductor of the people," coaching others on applying a conductor's sensibilities for personal and professional growth. According to Talgam, the orchestra conductor doesn't make a sound; their power lies in making other people powerful.

"The joy [of leadership]," Talgam says, "is about enabling other people's stories to be heard."

That is the ultimate servant: the quiet hand that leads others to be great, recognized, and applauded. Great leaders aspire to create a safe place where others can shine and everyone shares the spotlight.

Servant-leaders prioritize the growth and well-being of their team members, creating an environment that encourages open communication, trust, and collaboration. Leaders who genuinely care about their employees' well-being and development foster higher levels of engagement. They adopt a mindset and display behaviors that prioritize serving others, putting others' needs before their own, and working toward overall well-being and success. When employees feel valued, supported, and connected to their work's purpose, they are more likely to be motivated, dedicated, and satisfied with their jobs.

By empowering their team members and fostering a supportive culture, servant-leaders enable individuals to contribute their best efforts, share their ideas, and work together toward common goals. Serving others by helping them do things for the cause of overall good, instead of telling them what to do and how to do it, can be a leader's greatest gift.

A TINY MOMENT
Serve Up Support

One of my star employees at the ad agency was Alex. She was the epitome of an account executive. She had an uncanny ability to understand client needs, a knack for managing multiple projects, and a gift for building strong relationships. Clients loved working with her, and her colleagues admired her dedication and expertise. But even the best account executives have their moments of struggle.

At one point, we landed a large new client that was launching a revolutionary product. The stakes were high and the pressure was substantial. Alex led the account, and while she was excited, she soon found herself overwhelmed. The client was demanding, the deadlines were tight, and the team's workload was through the roof.

As I left work late one evening, I noticed the light still on in Alex's office. I walked over and found her slumped in her chair, surrounded by stacks of papers, her laptop open and emails stacked up. She looked exhausted, her usual confident demeanor replaced with stress and frustration. When I asked why she was there so late, Alex sighed and said, "I know, but there's just so much to do. This client is expecting miracles, and I don't want to let anyone down."

I immediately pulled up a chair, sat beside her, and told her that she was one of the best account executives I'd ever seen. I asked her how I could help. Alex looked at me, surprised. "You're the owner. You have a million things to worry about." I told her that I did and that one of those things was to make sure my team was supported and successful. I followed this with, "What do you need? Let's figure this out together."

For the next hour, Alex and I went through the project details. I listened intently, offering suggestions and helping Alex prioritize tasks. After our time together, she made a list of tasks she could delegate to others and even called in a favor from a freelancer she trusted to handle some of the smaller tasks.

As we worked together, Alex felt the weight lift off her shoulders. The Tiny Moment of me demonstrating my genuine willingness to help made all the difference. I didn't just offer solutions. I embodied the "heart of a servant," showing genuine care for my team's well-being. By the time we finished, it was late into the night, but Alex felt more confident and in control. She thanked me, saying she didn't know what she would have done without my help.

I assured her that's what I'm here for, that we're a team, and we support each other. The next day, she returned to the office with renewed energy. With my support and the team's collective effort, the team, led by Alex, navigated the project's challenges and delivered a campaign that exceeded the client's expectations.

From that day forward, Alex knew she could rely on me not just as a boss, but as a leader with the heart of a servant, always ready to lend a hand and support the team in any way I could.

CHAPTER FORTY

Wear the Right Hat

THERE IS a corollary to the servant leadership approach discussed in the previous chapter. The concept of "wearing the right hat" refers to the importance of understanding the nuances of the various situations encountered when looking for opportunities to

Tom's evolution from a rigid, one-size-fits-all leader to a dynamic, supportive, and adaptable figure serves as an inspiring example for all aspiring leaders.

help. Some team members will be struggling, some could just use some direction, and others will be highly competent and benefit from high-level thinking. Great power lies in the sensibility to meet people where they are and craft your approach to meet their specific needs in that moment.

Everyone possesses different abilities and is at a different stage of their careers. Depending on their skill level and the circumstances, they will respond most favorably to the leadership approach—or leadership hat—that best fits the specific situation.

Effective leadership is about having a rainbow hat that you can turn to reveal the color that fits the needs of the moment and the people before you. It's not one-size-fits-all; it's ever-changing, sometimes requiring different approaches within the same meeting or conversation. You must change your role to fit the needs of the moment.

You'll need to be a **general** when people are floundering. This calls for tough feedback delivered in a compassionate, clear, and straightforward way. It requires taking over the situation for a while, proactively leading conversations that result in solution-oriented thinking, and even specifically prescribing the next steps that need to be taken. In this leadership mode, you'll want to help people see the bigger picture, suggest possible options, and lead by example.

Take on the role of **coach** when people are motivated but lack direction. Coaching requires soft skills such as active listening, perception, empathy, and patience. Supervise them throughout the process, provide useful feedback, and clarify expectations. When people ask for answers rather than seek out solutions, deploy tactics that help them think in a more progressive way to find their own answers. For those employees with an interest in personal development, the coach will become a mentor in areas where they want to improve.

Back off to the role of a **captain** when people are competent, experienced, informed, and motivated. What is it that inspires each of your team members? By understanding the mentality of each player, you'll be able to better understand what's in it for them and use it to fuel their internal motivation. Perhaps you can help work through a conflict or an attachment to a certain way of working. As a captain, it's your job to gently guide employees to gain new perspectives and see different points of view.

Be a **friendly expert** when highly competent and motivated people need some facilitation. In this role, offer knowledge or information that helps move thoughts, ideas, and solutions down the road. You've been around longer, worked through more experiences, and gained a reservoir of expertise that put you in a position to offer breakthrough insights. These tidbits of knowledge can be the factor that connects the dots and frees thinking to go to the next level. Your input can be the key to a door that, when opened, reveals the next set of thoughts.

Recognize when it's time to switch hats by being present for your team, truly understanding them, and putting everything into context. At its core, wearing the right hat is an interpersonal role. To know when to choose your different hats, you must see the entire picture. It requires spending time with your team and reading the room. It's up to you to decide when one hat is not enough or is too heavy-handed and shift to another best suited for that circumstance.

Adapting to the Circumstances

During my tenure in Major League Baseball, I had the privilege of working with Tom, who served as our director of sales. Known for his strong reputation as a sports marketing professional, Tom consistently approached work situations with a structured and reliable methodology. However, as our business expanded so did his staff, which brought a diverse set of skills and needs into the mix. Tom's initial "one-size-fits-all" approach proved inadequate in addressing the variety of circumstances he now faced, necessitating a significant adaptation.

One pivotal day, Tom was closely observing his team as they navigated a complex issue. He realized they were capable but needed someone to listen and guide them. Instead of dictating solutions, Tom started facilitating their problem-solving process. He helped them identify issues, organize their thoughts, and develop solutions collaboratively. After a particularly productive brainstorming session, one team member, while leaving a side conversation about a recent football game, casually remarked to Tom, "Thanks, coach."

In that Tiny Moment, Tom understood the importance of "wearing the right hat." He recognized that his team members had potential but needed vision and cohesion. This revelation led Tom to shift his approach from providing direct answers to asking guiding questions and offering patient support. By doing so, he met his team members where they were, fostering their growth and development.

Tom's journey of transformation did not go unnoticed. We recognized the positive impact of his adaptive leadership style. His ability to adjust his role to meet the specific needs of each situation impressed the executive leadership of the team, leading to his promotion to a more senior leadership position within the organization. This advancement was not just a reward for his expertise in sales but a testament to his commitment to understanding and addressing the unique challenges and aspirations of his team members.

Sparked by the Tiny Moment that happened the day he saw his staff struggling, Tom transformed himself into a versatile leader, capable of seamlessly switching between the roles of a general, coach, captain, and friendly expert as circumstances demanded. This ability to adapt and connect with his team on various levels made him an invaluable asset to the organization.

Tom's story is a testament to the power of adaptability in leadership. His willingness to listen, learn, and change his approach not only enhanced his effectiveness but also fostered a more cohesive and capable team. Tom's evolution from a rigid, one-size-fits-all leader to a dynamic, supportive, and adaptable figure serves as an inspiring example for all aspiring leaders. His success is a reminder that authentic leadership is not about rigidly sticking to one method but about being perceptive, flexible, and responsive to the needs of the team and the challenges at hand. His journey highlights the importance of flexibility in leadership and the profound impact it can have on both personal growth and organizational success.

CHAPTER FORTY-ONE

The Purpose of Power
Is to Give It Away

TRANSFORMATION IS a theme in this book. To be transformational is, by definition, to "change in form, appearance, or character." It is the act of evolving and converting something to its next iteration. Let's face it—nothing ever stays the same. So it really comes down to how we embrace and guide these evolutions in our lives and the lives of those around us.

Letting go means allowing individuals to become independent and self-sufficient, enabling them to apply their knowledge and skills without constant supervision.

An organization evolves by people taking on more responsibility, higher-level work and leadership roles. This cannot happen if one or only a few top-level people hold on to power and fail to distribute authority to others. People will wait around until someone tells them what to do. Proactivity and take-charge behavior will atrophy without intervention. Bottlenecks will occur as everyone waits for the anointed ones to issue instructions.

Our days are full of questions and decisions. How we respond determines both our personal and business lives. I generally have opinions about almost anything that comes up in a day, but I can't foist my thoughts on those around me. Instead, I must ask others to weigh in.

I need everyone to know that they are not only free to offer their perspective, but I expect them to do so. They will only do this if they feel they have a position of authority, that their viewpoint matters, and they have the power to take a stand. Otherwise they will freeze and "turtle." As a result, the organization leaves good brain power on the sidelines and loses the potential firepower these people might bring to the table.

I often say, "I know we CAN. But SHOULD we?" when someone responds to a suggestion with, "We can do that," but has no opinion about the wisdom of that particular action. We don't gain much from having people confirm we have options; we always have options. The key is the thought process behind developing alternative options and then ultimately deciding on the best one.

As an example, let's say I suggest emailing an agenda before a meeting to ensure everyone is on the same page, and the response I get is, "Sure, we can do that." I will most likely respond (hopefully nicely and respectfully), "I know we can do that. We can do anything. I'm asking if spending time preparing an agenda in advance for this particular meeting is worth the time."

By putting the question back in others' courts, we establish an environment of authority and empowerment. You give power away by asking your team to feel invested with an opinion. You give them permission to think and to tell you what should be done and why. You are saying, "I am bestowing this power upon you. You no longer need to defer to me as a higher power here. You have the power."

All leaders need to act with "generous intent," actualizing their expertise and leadership capability by developing an organizational culture and a personal commitment to nurturing leadership capacity. An important aspect of leadership is "legacy"—what one leaves behind. Identifying and developing the next generation of leadership should be at the heart of what we as leaders contribute to any enterprise.

"Teach, mentor, let go" is a phrase that encapsulates a progressive approach to guiding and developing individuals. It emphasizes the importance of

THE PURPOSE OF POWER IS TO GIVE IT AWAY

imparting knowledge and skills, providing guidance and support, and ultimately allowing individuals to grow and flourish independently.

While teaching and mentoring are the foundational aspects of this approach, the final step of "letting go" can be the most difficult. Letting go means allowing individuals to become independent and self-sufficient, enabling them to apply their knowledge and skills without constant supervision. It involves giving them space to explore, make their own decisions, and learn from their mistakes. Letting go does not mean abandoning or neglecting individuals but rather giving them the freedom to develop their abilities and take ownership of their growth. It signifies trust in their capabilities and confidence in the lessons they have learned through your teaching and mentoring.

You don't lose power by sharing it, you multiply it.

A TINY MOMENT
Step Up to Step Aside

Sometimes Tiny Moments of change are inspired by necessity.

Dave, a senior creative leader at my ad agency, had a sharp, creative mind and impeccable work ethic. For years, he led his team of creatives with a firm yet inspiring hand, orchestrating every brainstorming session to churn out innovative ideas for high-profile clients. His approach was effective. He would start with a clear objective, lead the discussion, and ultimately guide his team toward the final concept. This method had produced many successful campaigns, and Dave took pride in his ability to steer the ship.

However, as our agency grew, so did the complexity and volume of projects. Dave found himself stretched thin, juggling numerous responsibilities while trying to maintain the same level of involvement in every brainstorming session. The energy in the room began to feel different—less vibrant and more pressured. It was clear to him that something needed to change.

One day, during a particularly spirited brainstorming session for a new campaign, Dave noticed Jen, a young and talented copywriter, had lots of ideas and enthusiasm. Jen had always contributed valuable insights, but that day, she seemed especially attuned to the task at hand. Midway through the session, in one Tiny Moment, Dave had an epiphany: Perhaps it was time to let someone else take the lead. With a deep breath, he looked around the room and then directly at Jen.

"Jen," Dave said, catching her off guard, "why don't you take the lead here?" As Dave nodded encouragingly, Jen stepped up. The dynamic shifted instantly. Jen's approach and style were different. She was fluid and open. She encouraged wild ideas and built on the team's spontaneous energy. The session became a vibrant exchange of creativity, and the team left the room buzzing with new concepts.

Over the next few weeks, Dave continued to let Jen lead the brainstorms. The change was profound. The team felt more empowered, their ideas flowed more freely, and the campaigns they produced began to reflect newfound originality and freshness. Dave watched from the sidelines, offering guidance when needed but largely allowing Jen to steer the creative ship.

In what started as a Tiny Moment, Dave discovered that letting go of the reins created several unexpected benefits. First, he noticed his stress levels decreasing. Without the constant pressure to direct every session, he had more time to focus on strategic planning and client relationships. This shift also allowed him to see his team members in a new light, recognizing talents and leadership qualities that he had previously overlooked.

Moreover, the team thrived under Jen's leadership. She brought a different perspective and energy to the sessions, which resonated with the younger team members. They felt heard and valued, and their creative confidence grew. The team's overall morale improved, and this positive energy transferred to their work, resulting in more innovative and effective campaigns.

Dave realized that by letting go of power, he had not only reduced his own burden but had also unlocked the full potential of his team. It was a humbling lesson in leadership: true leadership is not about holding on to control but about knowing when to step back and let others shine. By trusting Jen and the rest of his team, Dave had created an environment where creativity could flourish, and everyone felt empowered to contribute their best.

Dave's decision to relinquish control became a turning point for the agency. It fostered a culture of collaboration and innovation, proving that sometimes, the most powerful act of leadership is knowing when to let go.

CHAPTER FORTY-TWO

Celebrate Innovation

SOME LEADERS claim to love innovators but don't allow for the curiosity, playfulness, and failures that accompany successful innovation. This often comes from a lack of understanding of what it takes to create something new. They hear success stories and want those

As a leader, you must encourage innovative thinking and draw out the best in people.

kinds of successful thinkers on their teams but aren't willing to give them the breathing room they need to innovate. They expect innovators to show up, see a challenge, and quickly deliver a clever solution. And if the first couple of ideas don't work, they assume they've misinterpreted what this person can deliver.

As a leader, you must encourage innovative thinking and draw out the best in people. Watch for the ones who look like they want to step up but don't, or perhaps start to act but then stop themselves. Based on what you know of the person, casually approach them and invite a conversation. You might say, "You seem to have an idea. I'd love to hear about it. I don't care if it sounds ridiculous; if there's a spark of an idea, it might light the fire that we're looking for."

Courage and presence can be superpowers. Unfortunately, some people fear failure so much that they don't try to do things. But only in the doing does anything ever get accomplished. And this includes experimentation that leads to things not working.

Remember that not everything must be big at the start. You may have ambitious dreams of introducing something truly innovative to the marketplace, even disrupting an industry. However, starting small with tiny sparks of ideas and then building upon them little by little is most often the best way to succeed. Start by encouraging imagination and a free flow of conversation in team-oriented groups.

Albert Einstein famously said, "We can't solve problems with the same kind of thinking that we used when we created them." But this is precisely what most companies do. They apply the same approach that created the problem to finding the solution. Einstein highlights that critical problem-solving needs fresh and innovative thinking, suggesting that relying on the same mindset or methods that led to a problem is unlikely to yield effective solutions. Nonetheless, many companies fall into the trap of using familiar approaches when faced with challenges.

It is crucial for organizations to recognize this approach's limitations. By fostering a culture of innovation, embracing diverse perspectives, and equipping employees with creative problem-solving skills, companies can break free from this cycle and unlock new possibilities for effective problem-solving.

A TINY MOMENT
Business as Unusual

In 2003, while running the Manchester Monarchs ice hockey team, I had a memorable experience that underscored the importance of innovation and trusting your team. One day Jon, the Vice President of Sales, approached me with what sounded like a ridiculous idea. "We should have a Mullet Night," he declared with unwavering enthusiasm.

I stared at him, waiting for the punchline that never came. "That sounds dumb. What am I missing?" I asked.

Jon talked about how the mullet haircut has become a symbol of the rugged, blue-collar spirit often celebrated in ice hockey culture, with many players and fans embracing the haircut as a nod to the sport's gritty and unpretentious roots. He pointed to the mullet's "business in the front, party in the back" aesthetic as a representation of both the seriousness and the fun that characterizes the hockey community. He suggested we honor this by ordering 8,000 mullet wigs, distributing them to our fans, and creating a night-long celebration of the "Wisconsin Waterfall," as he amusingly called it. Although I wasn't convinced initially, Jon's enthusiasm and strategic thinking won me over. I decided to trust him and give him the green light.

The payoff was extraordinary. Mullet Night was a sensation, quickly becoming an instant classic. Major networks like Fox and ESPN picked up the story, giving us invaluable publicity. To this day, when people hear I ran the Monarchs, they reminisce about how much they loved Mullet Night. I even closed a prospective client deal after sending her four mullet wigs I still had in storage. While the mullets weren't the sole reason she became a client, they certainly added a memorable touch.

This experience highlighted a fundamental truth: Innovation is critical to success. In a highly competitive industry like sports entertainment, staying ahead of the curve requires embracing new and sometimes unconventional ideas. It started with one Tiny Moment of an idea I didn't understand, but I trusted the person who did and gave him room to run with it. The rest is Monarchs history.

Innovation is the lifeblood of any successful organization. It's not just about coming up with new ideas but also about fostering an environment where creativity can thrive. This means being open to suggestions from all levels of the organization and being willing to take calculated risks. It means, as Apple once advertised, to "Think Different." Jon's idea for Mullet Night was unconventional, but it tapped into the quirky, fun-loving spirit of hockey fans and created a unique experience that resonated deeply with our audience.

The same principle applies to leadership in any field. Effective leaders recognize the value of empowering their team members to explore and implement innovative ideas. This involves stepping back and allowing others to take the lead, much like Dave did at the ad agency by letting Jen run the brainstorming sessions. By doing so, leaders can unlock the full potential of their teams, fostering a culture of collaboration and creativity.

For the Monarchs, Mullet Night wasn't just a promotional success; it was a testament to the power of innovation and the importance of trusting your team. It showed me that even the most seemingly outlandish ideas could lead to remarkable outcomes if given the chance. This lesson in innovation and trust has stayed with me throughout my career, reminding me that the key to success often lies in the willingness to embrace the new and unexpected.

CHAPTER FORTY-THREE

FAILing Forward

FAILING AT things in life is
necessary to achieve our full
potential. We can exist without
failure, but we cannot grow without it. Failure is important, because
in failing, you gain new information,
understanding, and ideas.

*The art of failing forward
is learning how to
overcome failure and
bounce back.*

Learn to love and log failure. Pay attention to it. Dig for the gold in the
rubble, because I guarantee you it exists, and there's always something to
gain from trying. Encourage others to do the same.

Failing forward confirms that you are striving to grow and do things
better. You're risking and daring and wanting. You're trying new things you
have never tried before. You can't fail if you're not trying, so getting in and
taking your swings demonstrates effort. And in a world where 85 percent
of life is just showing up, you're already ahead of the game by getting in
there and doing things. "You miss 100 percent of the shots you don't take,"
Wayne Gretzky famously said.

I'm not talking about massive, catastrophic failures. I'm talking about
smaller, more common mini-failures based on "commission" instead of
"omission." Failure by commission refers to failure resulting from acting,
while failure by omission refers to failure from not acting or neglecting

to fulfill expected responsibilities. While both types of failures can have significant consequences, failure by commission is far more acceptable if the decision was made based on research, data, and smart analysis of the risk-reward proposition at hand.

Often, when we fail, we pout, feel defeated, are embarrassed—or maybe scream. We second-guess that we even tried it in the first place. When something doesn't work, you think with a heavy sigh, "Back to square one." But the reality is, you're not going back to the very beginning because the beginning was the unknown. So, even if something seems like a 100 percent failure, you are always at least a little ahead of where you started. You now know what doesn't work. It might not always feel like it, but you're always failing forward because you're learning.

The story goes that Thomas Edison invented the light bulb after making 1,000 unsuccessful attempts. When a reporter asked him how it felt to fail 1,000 times, he reportedly replied, "I didn't fail 1,000 times. The light bulb was an invention with 1,000 steps."

Like Edison, the art of failing forward is learning how to overcome failure and bounce back. It can have a profound impact on resilience, personal growth, and success. Developing resilience enables you to face future obstacles with confidence and adaptability. As the common maxim holds, "Our greatest glory is not in never falling, but in rising every time we fall."

Steve Jobs is one of the best examples of someone who approached failure as a catalyst for growth and innovation. He viewed failures as valuable learning experiences, embraced them as part of the journey, and used them to fuel his determination to succeed. By leveraging failure in these ways, he played a pivotal role in transforming multiple industries and left a lasting legacy. The Apple III computer, the NEXT company, and an unceremonious firing as the head of Apple are some of the failures Jobs faced. He used these failures as a powerful motivator for his continued work and to prove his detractors wrong. He was driven by a desire to show resilience and demonstrate that setbacks did not define him. This motivation fueled his determination to succeed and create products that would shape the future.

One thing is for sure—this is not a new concept. In 1840, Thomas H. Palmer published the prized essay "The Teacher's Manual: Being an Exposition of an Efficient and Economical System of Education, Suited to the Wants of a Free People."[1] In his essay, Thomas wrote the very famous motivational proverb:

'Tis a lesson you should heed, Try, try again;
If at first you don't succeed, Try, try again.

A TINY MOMENT
Learn to Fail or Fail to Learn

During my tenure as the president of the Manchester Monarchs in the American Hockey League (AHL), I had the privilege of witnessing numerous extraordinarily talented athletes on their path to the National Hockey League (NHL). It was evident that a critical component of their training was mastering the art of coping with the emotional toll of small failures. In the world of professional sports, where the margin for error is razor-thin, learning how to handle failure was an essential skill for these aspiring NHL players. While their primary goal was to secure a spot in the big leagues, the minor pro leagues offer an opportunity to learn how to handle failure in front of smaller crowds before they faced the scorn of failing in front of a sold-out NHL arena of 20,000 disappointed fans.

One such athlete was a young goalie named Carter. Fresh out of junior hockey, Carter was brimming with talent and potential but soon found that the transition to professional hockey was fraught with challenges. In his first season with the Monarchs, Carter faced numerous setbacks. Every mistake was magnified in his mind, and the pressure to perform was immense. During one particularly tough game, Carter allowed several goals, leading to a defeat for the team. As the crowd expressed their disappointment, Carter felt the weight of failure bearing down on him.

However, this was where the true value of the minor league experience and a Tiny Moment of discovery came into play. Carter's coach pulled him aside after the game. Instead of reprimanding him, Bruce shared stories of his own struggles and failures, emphasizing that even the greatest players had endured similar moments. He explained that the minor leagues were a proving ground, a place to learn and grow without the intense scrutiny of the NHL spotlight.

The wisdom shared in the Tiny Moment was like a light bulb being turned on, inspiring Carter to start viewing his failures not as insurmountable obstacles but as opportunities for growth. He worked tirelessly in practice, focusing on his weaknesses and refining his skills. His teammates rallied around him, providing support and encouragement. Slowly but surely, Carter's confidence began to rebuild. He started to see each game, each save, and even each mistake as a step on his journey to becoming a better goalie.

Carter learned that failure was not a foe but a faithful companion in the pursuit of greatness. His journey from the minor leagues to the NHL was a story of grit, resilience, and the power of learning from failure. It was a clear representation of how leaders can help others understand that the true measure of success lies not in the absence of failure but in the courage to face it head-on and emerge even stronger on the other side.

CHAPTER FORTY-FOUR

Recognize and Celebrate

MARY KAY Ash, the founder of Mary Kay Cosmetics, once said, "There are two things people want more than sex and money: recognition and praise."

Recognition is universally shown to amplify well-being in ways that make a noticeable impact. It makes employees feel their organization recognizes their work and truly cares about them. It can be the difference between

Regularly acknowledge achievements, both big and small, and don't wait for special occasions to do it.

a good day or a bad day, a good week or a bad week at work. When people are happy and feel part of a team, the product is always better.

Recognition is essential today as younger generations join the workforce. Gallup found that younger employees (Gen Z and younger millennials) are 73 percent more likely than their older counterparts to want recognition at least a few times a month.[1]

In a 2019 study by daVinci Payments, 70 percent of Gen Z and millennials said they would stay on in their job for another year if they received three $50 prepaid awards in a year.[2] Imagine: Only $150 per employee per year to motivate, improve engagement, and slow employee churn!

Another study conducted by Nectar underscores the critical role of recognition in workplace satisfaction and motivation. According to the findings, an overwhelming 87 percent of employees report that meaningful recognition significantly impacts their job satisfaction. The study also highlights that regular acknowledgment of contributions fosters a positive work environment, leading to improved morale, engagement, and productivity. Lack of recognition, conversely, can lead to disengagement and high turnover rates.[3] These statistics reinforce the necessity for leaders to prioritize consistent and personalized recognition strategies, demonstrating that even small acts of appreciation can yield substantial benefits for both employees and organizations.

Bottom line: Recognized employees are happy employees.

A large-scale 2022 Gallup study of more than 12,000 employees showed that fulfilling employee recognition correlates to better employee well-being across several key areas. The study found that recognition lifts spirit, reduces level of burnout, and improves daily emotion. It goes on to state that "employees who strongly agree that they get the right amount of recognition for the work they do are up to 84 percent more likely to be thriving. And when employees give recognition at work at least a few times a month, they are as much as two times more likely to be thriving than those who don't."[4]

According to the study, "When organizations create an environment in which employees consistently receive high-quality recognition, these benefits—and more—translate into clear ROI [return on investment]. To do this, leaders must first see recognition as a strategy that needs to be invested in and then scale it thoughtfully to change the culture of their workplaces and, ultimately, employees' lives."

Dale Carnegie agreed, "People work for money but go the extra mile for recognition, praise and rewards."

Amplifying the wellness of your employees through recognition must be authentic and personalized, distributed fairly, and embedded in the culture. Regularly acknowledge achievements, both big and small, and don't wait for special occasions to do it. Celebrate employee work anniversaries, birthdays, and other personal milestones to demonstrate that you care about them as individuals, not just as workers.

Recognition is a contagious spark that ignites positivity throughout the workplace. When one person takes the time to genuinely acknowledge and celebrate the achievements of a colleague, it sets off a chain reaction, inspiring others to follow suit and creating a culture where appreciation flows freely and organically.

The ripple effect of recognition creates a culture where appreciation and encouragement become the norm, leading to a more motivated and engaged workforce. Ultimately, the contagious nature of recognition fuels an environment where everyone strives for their best and celebrates each other's accomplishments, making the workplace an infinitely more positive and harmonious environment.

Demonstrating appreciation by recognizing employees is the spark that ignites motivation and excellence within an organization. It's an acknowledgement that every individual's actions, no matter how small, contribute to the collective success of the team. When we celebrate our employees, we not only illuminate their path but also light the way for our collective success.

As Jim Goodnight, CEO of SAS Institute, an analytics software company, says, "Treat employees like they make a difference, and they will."

A TINY MOMENT

Identify. Recognize. Celebrate. Repeat.

I am a big advocate for leaders finding Tiny Moments to call attention to someone going above and beyond. One effective way to do this is through internal chat channels. For example, at my advertising agency, we have a page dedicated to "A-Players," where everyone can recognize another for doing something noteworthy.

It started as small shout-outs, but quickly evolved to an "A-Player of the Month," where the people who get the most mentions are recognized and rewarded with a gift card. The launch of the A-player page felt like a Tiny Moment in itself; it went to the next level when we started giving gift cards to the people who voted the most, expanding the recognition to also honor the people who were most engaged in the appreciation process. It is not just about celebrating the people who do great work; it's also about recognizing the cheerleaders.

It's awesome to see the impact these Tiny Moments have on the energy and esprit de corps in the office. They not only give the recipients an occasion to shine, but each and every A-player shout-out also inspires the entire organization. The messages in the A-player chat channel are always the first ones everyone wants to read. Imagine that. One tiny comment, most often fewer than fifty words, lifts up an entire organization. It's a cherished, tiny, feel-good occasion.

The timing of recognition is crucial. We had a member of our sales team who scored an unexpected win for our organization. Instead of immediately congratulating her, I remembered that we had an after-work social gathering that day. In that Tiny Moment, I decided to hold my congratulations until it could be shared in front of the entire organization. With everyone together, I took a moment to thank her for bringing in a new client. She was beaming, and that made me very happy for her and everyone who was there.

Recognizing efforts through Tiny Moments unlocks the transformative power of acknowledging and appreciating accomplishments, both big and small. Whether it's the A-player shout-outs on our internal chat channels or the strategic timing of celebrating unexpected wins during after-work social gatherings, these Tiny Moments foster a sense of camaraderie and elevate the collective spirit of the organization.

The ripple effect of recognizing not only outstanding work but also the cheerleaders within the team emphasizes the importance of creating a positive and uplifting work environment, where every tiny comment becomes a cherished feel-good occasion that resonates throughout the entire organization.

CHAPTER FORTY-FIVE

Praise in Public, Criticize in Private

OKAY, SO we've covered the positives of recognizing people for their good work and doing it in a celebratory way. Now, how about when it comes time to have the not-so-good conversation when things need improvement?

Criticism can be hard to accept, but when properly delivered, it can be a catalyst for change and improved performance. Winston Churchill concisely illustrated this concept when he said, "Criticism may not be agreeable, but it is necessary. It fulfills the same function as pain in the human body: it calls attention to the development of an unhealthy state of things."[1]

Public criticism tends to trigger a defensive reaction that makes it much harder for a person to accept their mistake and learn from it.

Still, our very wiring as human beings works against us in handling criticism. Psychological research shows that our brain must experience five positive events to make up for the psychological effect of just one negative event. We all want and need to feel good about ourselves, so the moment someone judges us negatively, any doubts we may have about ourselves can immediately rise to the surface.

A good rule of thumb for feedback is to praise in public, criticize in private.

Public recognition boosts the individual's self-esteem and motivation, and the morale of the entire team. Celebrating positivity in the open and with the group is a good thing, as it shows that their efforts are appreciated and valued. Recognizing accomplishments in front of peers reinforces the behavior you want to encourage, fostering a positive and productive work environment. Public praise fosters trust among team members by demonstrating that hard work and dedication are recognized and rewarded. Celebrating successes together fosters a sense of camaraderie within the team and encourages others to emulate whatever was done that was worthy of praise.

On the other hand, criticism in public, even when constructive, is generally embarrassing. Public criticism tends to trigger a defensive reaction that makes it much harder for a person to accept their mistake and learn from it.

You will make much more progress talking in private. Privately discussing challenges or constructive feedback respects the individual's dignity and avoids potentially embarrassing situations. It encourages more honest and open conversations and provides a chance to offer guidance, provide context, and discuss growth opportunities. Privately addressing issues reduces the likelihood of conflicts escalating in a public setting, which can harm relationships and teamwork.

I learned this one the hard way as a young leader. I am open and transparent, so I tend to say what I think. This can be positive; one perspective is that we could use more "tell it like it is" conversations to cut to the chase and get things done more efficiently. However, over time we learn that style, tone, and timing have a great deal to do with effective relationships and communication. You start to get the idea when you create interpersonal problems by making a mistake in how, when, and/or where you communicate.

How often have we said—or been told—"Not now. It's not the right time." Timing is everything no matter what the message, but especially when it is critical. Author Joshua Harris says, "The right thing at the wrong time is the wrong thing."[2]

Incorporating "praise in public, criticize in private" into your communication style helps create a balanced approach that maintains positive relationships while addressing areas that need improvement. It fosters a culture of respect, transparency, and growth within teams and organizations.

A TINY MOMENT
Take a Beat Before You Speak

Early in my career, I had a valuable learning moment that shaped my approach to leadership. It happened with a young employee named Jake, who had recently joined our team. Jake was eager, hardworking, and full of potential, but like anyone, he made occasional mistakes.

One afternoon, Jake made an error on a project that had significant implications for a customer. Frustrated by the situation and driven by the urgency to correct it, I discussed the issue with Jake in front of some members of the team. My intention was to address the mistake quickly and ensure it didn't happen again, but I failed to consider the impact of my approach.

Jake's face turned red as I pointed out his mistake. He nodded, apologized, and assured me he would fix it immediately. The room was silent, but I was too focused on resolving the issue to think much about it. The rest of the day passed without incident, and by the time I left the office, I felt the problem had been adequately addressed.

The next morning, Jake knocked on my office door. He looked nervous but determined, and he asked if I had a minute to talk. I said, "Of course," expecting him to discuss the project.

He closed the door behind him and took a seat. "I wanted to talk to you about yesterday," he began hesitantly. "When you reprimanded me in front of everyone, it made me feel embarrassed and intimidated. I know I made a mistake, and I'm sorry for that. But being called out like that in front of my colleagues was really tough."

His words hit me hard. I hadn't realized the impact of my actions. I had accomplished my goal of addressing the mistake quickly, but in my haste, I had inadvertently humiliated Jake in front of his peers. I felt a pang of guilt when I saw the hurt in his eyes.

I sincerely apologized to Jake, telling him that I was so focused on fixing the issue that I handled the situation poorly. I thanked him for having the courage to come and talk to me about it.

Jake nodded, his expression softening. "I appreciate that. It's important to me to learn and grow, but I need to feel supported, not singled out."

This conversation was a pivotal Tiny Moment for me. I realized that as a leader, my words and actions had a significant impact on my team. I needed to create an environment where employees felt safe and respected, even when mistakes were made.

From that day forward, I adopted the principle of "praise in public, criticize in private." I made a conscious effort to address issues privately and to recognize achievements publicly. This approach not only helped build a more positive and supportive team culture but also strengthened my relationships with my employees.

Jake's Tiny Moment of honesty and courage taught me a valuable lesson about leadership. By handling criticism with care and empathy, I could foster a more productive and motivated team. The experience reminded me that leadership is not just about driving results but also about nurturing and supporting the people who contribute to those results.

CHAPTER FORTY-SIX

Change Demands Compromise

I N T H E chapter "If It Ain't Broke, Break It," we discussed that while most people dislike and avoid change, it is necessary for professional and personal growth.

> *A willingness to compromise builds trust between a leader and a team.*

Professor Irwin Corey said, "If we don't change direction soon, we'll end up where we're going." The critical part of that quote for our discussion is "we." Change involves a team, and to change direction together, someone or something will have to compromise, so you must include everyone.

The successful delivery of change may hinge on front-line managers and supervisors, but it involves all who touch on the project along the way. It might even include people who don't directly touch it but influence the people who do. Anyone in or adjacent to this circle of change can be a positive or negative influence on successful implementation. Therefore, considering how everyone will respond to change and how to influence this response has a powerful impact on success.

When you ask yourself the "why" and "how" instead of only the "what," the concept of compromise emerges. Compromise is vital in facilitating change because it allows different perspectives and interests to be reconciled, leading to progress and forward movement. It is crucial for facilitating change by building consensus, balancing competing interests, fostering collaboration, and helping overcome resistance. By embracing compromise, organizations and societies can navigate change more effectively and achieve outcomes that address a broader range of perspectives and needs.

An approach focused on compromise creates "bottom-up change," where everyone on the team feels heard and valued when faced with challenges. This leads to employees having a say in meeting the challenge.

Compromise also helps ensure the company and its leaders stay true to values. Many companies claim to care about their employees, and it's easy to see this as true when things are running smoothly. However, the way a company treats its staff during challenging times truly reveals how it feels about the people it employs. Making demands that offer no alternatives or not exhibiting a willingness to discuss options devalues the people who matter the most.

A willingness to compromise builds trust between a leader and a team. If you, as the leader, are willing to listen and work with an employee and help them figure out a solution sparked by their own idea, when something else comes up down the line that creates a similar challenge, they are more likely to give priority to making it work. You respected them before, so they want to help you now as a show of respect and gratitude.

And who knows, through the process of compromise, you might find other solutions that can benefit the company in the future.

A TINY MOMENT
Compromise Is a Win-Win

Establishing and living by organizational core values has always been a priority for me. At one point, we were revisiting and updating these values at the ad agency. The core value of focusing on "Innovation" was of particular interest. I proposed we adopt the mantra, "If it ain't broke, break it," a provocative twist on the familiar saying, "If it ain't broke, don't fix it." My intention was to inspire a mindset of constant improvement and fearless innovation.

However, this bold approach was met with resistance. Mary, one of our team members, was particularly averse to the notion of deliberately breaking things that were functioning well. Her perspective was rooted in the hard work and dedication we had invested in building effective solutions to problems. To her, the idea of actively seeking to break these accomplishments was counterproductive and demotivating.

Mary's reaction was understandable. She was proud of the work we had done and saw the value in maintaining efficient systems and processes. The concept of breaking them for the sake of innovation seemed reckless and unnecessary. Her concerns highlighted an important aspect of change management: respecting the emotional and psychological investment people have in their work.

Recognizing the need for a balanced approach, I initiated a conversation with Mary to understand her perspective better. I explained that the mantra wasn't about destroying our successes but rather about being open to challenging the status quo. There were undoubtedly areas within our operations that, while seemingly functional, could benefit from a fresh perspective or a radical overhaul. The essence of innovation lies in the willingness to question, re-evaluate, and improve continuously.

During this Tiny Moment discussion, it became clear that change is best accomplished through compromise. I suggested tweaking the statement to this: "Be open to breaking things that do not appear to be broken." This slight modification maintained the spirit of the original mantra while addressing Mary's concerns. It conveyed the idea of proactive improvement without implying a disregard for the efforts and successes we had achieved.

Mary accepted this revised statement, and it was adopted as our guiding principle for innovation. This experience underscored the importance of involving team members in the process of defining core values and compromise. By incorporating their perspectives and addressing their concerns, we were able to craft a statement that accurately reflected our commitment to innovation.

The journey of refining our core value of innovation taught me that effective leadership requires both vision and empathy. It's about inspiring bold ideas while also respecting the collective achievements of the team. Ultimately, our new mantra encouraged a culture of continuous improvement and openness to change, which became a cornerstone of our agency's success.

CHAPTER FORTY-SEVEN

Make Their Personal Vision Yours

HELPING PEOPLE ignite their passion is helping them find fulfillment. You can gather people around a vision, but creating "glue" involves helping individuals strive toward what they want and working with them to find personal achievement. People recognize and appreciate those around

When people achieve their aspirations, they often seek to pay it forward, creating a chain reaction of positive influence.

them who genuinely are interested in their personal goals and dreams. The true magic happens when these personal aspirations harmonize with those of the business.

We all want to attract and keep the best people. One way we do this is to help our people grow by nurturing their personal visions. People know if and when they're ready to move on, and that's okay. But while they're with us, we need to ensure they keep growing. People want to be seen, respected, and given opportunities to learn and advance.

It's one thing to say you want to attract the best people. Of course you do. No one is on the hunt for mediocrity. But how do you not only bring them in but also make them stay? It's by being truly 100 percent committed to their growth as whole people and knowing that this orientation will also serve the goal of company growth.

Consider it an honor and duty to be entrusted by people to make a difference in their lives, and take this opportunity very seriously. Be a facilitator between people and their dreams. While you cannot get someone from a junior level to a department head in one year, you can certainly help them get closer.

Caring about the dreams and visions of others creates a foundation of respect and forges strong and lasting relationships. Your support creates a bond built on shared goals and achievements. Those you help will likely feel grateful for your assistance, leading to a positive feedback loop of kindness and goodwill. When people achieve their aspirations, they often seek to pay it forward, creating a chain reaction of positive influence.

Helping someone achieve their dreams can bring immense satisfaction and a sense of accomplishment. Knowing that you played a role in their success is deeply fulfilling. It also fuels your growth by enhancing your communication, leadership, and mentoring skills. Witnessing others pursue their dreams can inspire and motivate you. Their determination and achievements can serve as a reminder of the potential for success in your endeavors.

I have always included a "personal vision" section in annual reviews. After covering all the areas of success and potential improvement, it is so important for me to know what they want in life. We spend quality time discussing this and, in many cases, I become involved in helping clarify and evolve these dreams. Over time, this became a central element of my leadership style.

A TINY MOMENT
Unlock the Potential of Your Team

Janie, a young woman with potential, joined our agency team as a traffic coordinator. Over time, her performance in this position was exemplary, and she seemed like a perfect fit. Given her competence and reliability, our plan was to retain her in this role as long as possible. Yet we realized that to truly harness Janie's potential and align it with the company's long-term goals, we needed to delve deeper into her personal aspirations.

A pivotal Tiny Moment unfolded during a performance review meeting between Janie and her supervisor, which I attended. As the conversation progressed, we discovered that she had an interest in pursuing a more advanced project manager professional track. Although she didn't fully understand the intricacies of this advanced role, she was drawn to the work she saw people with this title doing. Part of me wanted to keep her in her current role for a while, as it filled a crucial void in our workflow. However, I knew that responding to her aspirations was not only an investment in her future but could also complement the company's long-term staffing plans.

I acknowledged Janie's ambition and immediately began a conversation with her about what that path would look like. Frankly, I think she was surprised by my quick and positive response, but I recognized it as a valuable opportunity to demonstrate that I wanted to make her vision my vision.

From that moment on, we embarked on a journey of mutual growth. The agency provided Janie with the necessary resources and guidance. We integrated her personal goals into future one-on-one meetings, using these sessions as platforms for her to learn, grow, and refine her skills as a project manager. We established a structured development plan that included mentorship from experienced project managers, access to relevant training programs, and opportunities to shadow ongoing projects. This holistic approach ensured that Janie gained both theoretical knowledge and practical experience.

Janie diligently applied herself to the learning process, absorbing every bit of information and seeking feedback to continually improve. Her progress was remarkable, and her confidence grew with each passing day. Over time, she took on more responsibilities, gradually transitioning from her traffic coordinator duties to project management tasks.

Eventually, Janie did become a project manager—and a very good one at that. Her journey from traffic coordinator to project manager not only showcased her personal growth but also underscored the importance of nurturing talent within the organization.

Unlocking the true potential of those around you involves believing in their aspirations, supporting their growth, and encouraging their dreams to flourish. Make their vision your vision by aligning your goals with theirs. Demonstrate unwavering support and actively work toward their success as if it were your own. In doing so, you empower individuals to reach new heights and contribute to the collective success and resilience of your organization.

Janie's story is a testament to the transformative power of supportive leadership. By investing in her development and aligning her career path with the company's objectives, we not only helped Janie achieve her dreams but also strengthened our team with a skilled and motivated project manager.

CHAPTER FORTY-EIGHT

Take Fun Seriously

H ERE'S AN adage I can do without: "It's not supposed to be fun.
That's why they call it work."

There's a mistaken belief in today's
working world that leaders need to be
serious all the time to be taken seriously;
if we take our mission seriously, humor
somehow detracts from that mission. But
research tells a different story. According to
Stanford lecturers, leaders with a good sense
of humor are viewed as being 27 percent
more motivating.[1]

When people have fun and laugh together, they share a moment of vulnerability and connection that can strengthen their professional relationships.

When we laugh, our brains release hormones that make us feel calmer, more euphoric, and bonded. When we are having fun, engaging feels less risky, so laughing together results in feeling more connected. Humor is disarming. It lightens the mood, puts people at ease, and reduces the intimidation factor that powerful leaders can sometimes face. It demonstrates humility and shows you don't take yourself too seriously. The balance of gravity and levity gives power to both.

Fun can be described as something imaginative, lively, playful, and guided by rules that leave room for creativity. Appropriate humor might include laughter in meetings, personalized notes and gifts, spontaneous activities, or courteous frivolity. Whatever form it takes, fun is a secret weapon that builds bonds, power, creativity, and resilience. It helps to alleviate the self-conscious, judgmental inner voice that can make us feel reserved, restrained, and risk averse.

Suppressing these inhibitors can allow more freedom of thought and spark new possibilities. Playfulness invites us to adopt a childlike or beginner's mind that can encourage unfettered imagination. It utilizes creative rules that are different from regular life and permits people to do and say things they are not necessarily experts about.

While commonplace managers might push to "get back to work," inspiring leaders understand that work can sometimes feel and act like play. Cultivating an enjoyable atmosphere provides both tangible and intangible benefits that supersede keeping your head down and plowing through work. So, if you notice that organic fun is arising and everyone is enjoying themselves, it very well may be worth stepping back quietly and allowing it to happen rather than worrying about work that is not getting done at that very moment.

A word of caution: There can be a downside risk associated with fun and laughter in the workplace if you let it go too far. Behavior that causes others harm—even when meant to be playful—must be recognized and stopped.

However, when proper and innocuous humor exists, it is a positive force in the workplace. A study conducted at the University of Auckland found that fun at work can improve camaraderie, foster positive feelings, and boost engagement.[2] This sense of playfulness can transform the work environment, making it both more productive and enjoyable. It fosters connections, reduces stress, and enhances creativity, making work more enjoyable and productive.

Leaders should embrace fun in the workplace, recognizing its potential to transform the work environment for the better. When employees experience enjoyment at work, they are more likely to connect with one another and feel invested in their tasks.

Simply put, work doesn't work without play.

A TINY MOMENT
Take a Time-Out

I recall a time at the advertising agency when we had a big new business pitch to make, and a newly assembled creative team was assigned to work on the project. They were behind schedule on the day before they were to present their ideas internally. When I was leaving work to head home, I noticed they were settling in to work into the night.

As I made my way out, I touched base with Marlene, the team leader on this assignment. She told me she sensed some creative stress in the group and had an idea she hoped would help with this. It was not a ground-breaking idea for the creative product they were working on, but rather a tiny idea that would have a big, positive impact on getting that creative work done. The moment that she had the idea, she was on the phone ordering Ben & Jerry's ice cream to be delivered to the office.

When it arrived, Marlene told everyone to put down their work and meet in the kitchen. There the team found the most wonderful collection of ice cream treats they could imagine. They dug in joyously. And Marlene didn't rush the fun—the group stayed in the kitchen eating ice cream for a full thirty minutes.

Humor and fun in the workplace are not just about making people laugh. They are about creating an atmosphere where employees feel comfortable and relaxed so that they can be themselves and take risks. When people have fun and laugh together, they share a moment of vulnerability and connection that can strengthen their professional relationships.

Marlene's impromptu Tiny Moment worked. The team returned to their desks refreshed and clear-minded. This simple act of fun did more than provide a brief respite; it rejuvenated the team. The advertising business, like many others, is high-pressure and deadline-driven. The resulting stress can stifle creativity and decrease productivity. Marlene's actions demonstrated how leaders can incorporate fun as a powerful stress reliever.

Leaders should take note of this Tiny Moment lesson. Encouraging moments of levity and relaxation can be a game-changer for team dynamics and productivity. By breaking the monotony and easing the stress, Marlene was able to create an environment where her team felt revitalized and ready to go the extra mile and collaborate effectively. It was more than just a fun break; it was a strategic move that showcased the power of incorporating humor and fun into the workplace.

CHAPTER FORTY-NINE

Feedback Is a Gift

PRETTY MUCH every topic we've covered in this book, concepts like abundance, transformation, and trusting with verification, has a common thread—ongoing two-way communication.

How many times have you heard someone, when asked about issues at work, say that "poor communication" is the source of the problem? I have always thought this a very broad-brush observation because "communication"

In contrast to formal feedback structures, such as performance evaluations or disciplinary meetings, casual feedback can make individuals feel more comfortable and open to receiving input.

can refer to so many different things. When you break that word down, you realize that many everyday activities at work could contribute toward improved communication. Doing this makes us realize that none is more powerful than personal feedback.

It is not revolutionary to say that providing feedback to employees is important. We know it intuitively, and studies confirm it. Constructive feedback enhances performance, clarifies expectations, and promotes loyalty.

As author Ken Blanchard notes, "Feedback is the breakfast of champions."[1]

Effective feedback is essential in an employee's learning journey: It helps them better understand expectations and illuminates the path toward desired performance. It constructively deals with underperformance and contributes to higher levels of competence and confidence at all stages of their professional careers.

Failing to provide regular feedback comes at a cost. When employees are left to assess their performance in a vacuum, they will generally continue working in the same way. They know no better. This most often leads to an inaccurate assessment of their skills, building up a false perception of their abilities and performance.

We often deliver feedback in formal one-on-ones and performance reviews. These are important for official documentation purposes. Treat performance reviews with dignity and respect if you want to elevate them to something meaningful, helpful, and inspiring.

If an employee has poor behavior, less-than-adequate performance, or attitude problems, don't wait a year to fix them. Regular, ongoing coaching cannot be replaced with an annual employee review. Equally important are the casual interactions and spontaneous conversations that take place on a day-to-day basis.

Casual feedback, when provided in a non-threatening and non-confrontational manner, can be an effective tool in breaking down defensiveness. Leaders provide this feedback in an informal setting, such as during a chance conversation or in a relaxed environment. This approach helps create a less intimidating atmosphere and reduces the perception of a personal attack. In contrast to formal feedback structures, such as performance evaluations or disciplinary meetings, casual feedback can make individuals feel more comfortable and open to receiving input. The timeliness of these conversations also helps individuals connect the feedback to their actions, making it more relevant and actionable.

With all feedback:

- Make it effective by incorporating true, detailed reviews of what is going on.

- Listen to wants, needs, and challenges.

- Ask for improvement advice.

- Invite constructive criticism.

- Outline goals and create game plans that are continuously evaluated, updated, and checked on.

A TINY MOMENT
Don't Make Your Team Starve for Feedback

Ticket sales are the lifeblood of professional sports teams. When I joined the Milwaukee Brewers, our primary emphasis was to increase season ticket sales significantly.

Matt, the young manager of season ticket sales, was known for his sales skills and dedication to the organization. He was at the helm of steering our sales team toward meeting targets. Unfortunately, one of Matt's team members, Sarah, was underperforming—delivering subpar work and missing her goals. As Matt felt the pressure of hitting the team's ambitious season ticket total, he knew all team members had to deliver at a high level. He knew he had to address Sarah's performance, but he was unsure how to approach the situation without causing tension or demoralizing her.

One day, as Matt was sharing Sarah's issues with me, I told him something I had learned from one of my mentors. "No one should be surprised when they are fired for poor performance," I said. "Everyone deserves the benefit of feedback to help them be better."

During this Tiny Moment of insight, Matt realized he had not been giving his team, especially Sarah, the feedback they needed to improve. He decided to take a proactive approach and have a one-on-one conversation with Sarah.

The next morning, Matt invited Sarah to his office. She walked in, her demeanor defensive, clearly expecting a reprimand. Matt greeted her warmly and asked her to sit down. He started the conversation by acknowledging her hard work and dedication to the team. Then, he gently transitioned to discussing the areas where she was struggling. He respectfully told her she was capable of a higher quality of work. "I want you to know that I'm not here to reprimand you," Matt said, "but to understand how I can help you improve."

Sarah looked surprised but relieved. She opened up about the challenges she was facing and how she was feeling overwhelmed by the workload. Matt listened intently, realizing that he had not understood the factors impacting her work.

Matt expressed appreciation for Sarah's honesty and set up a plan to work together to find a solution. He set up a weekly check-in to go over tasks and discuss where she might need additional support. Visibly relieved, Sarah thanked him, telling him she had been feeling lost and didn't know how to ask for help.

Over the next few weeks, Matt made it a point to check in with Sarah regularly, providing constructive feedback and guidance. He also encouraged the rest of the team to support each other and foster a more collaborative environment. Slowly but surely, Sarah's performance began to improve. The quality of her work was higher, and she started meeting her goals. In fact, the overall morale of the team lifted as everyone saw the positive changes and felt supported.

Matt's small act of taking the time to provide feedback and support had made a significant impact. It reinforced his belief that effective leadership isn't just about driving results but, in the process, nurturing the people who achieve those results. By giving Sarah the feedback she needed, he not only helped her improve but also strengthened the entire team's cohesion and performance.

From that moment on, Matt made it a point to regularly give his team members constructive feedback and support, ensuring that no one was ever surprised by their performance reviews. His approach fostered a culture of continuous improvement and open communication, which ultimately led to our reaching the highest season ticket sales total in Brewers history.

CHAPTER FIFTY

Expect Growth

A GALLUP REPORT published in 2016 reveals that "87 percent of millennials rate 'professional or career growth and development opportunities' as important to them in a job."[1] They want to be useful and expand their knowledge and skills.

> *The best companies understand that true success lies in weaving professional growth into the very fabric of their culture.*

Professional growth helps people learn new skills that will support their career advancement. It provides opportunities to work on areas of weakness and to stay up to date on relevant knowledge. Acknowledging and supporting professional growth demonstrates that an employer is committed to the employee's career and willing to take steps to advance it.

The best companies understand that true success lies in weaving professional growth into the very fabric of their culture. When employees are given the opportunity to grow, they ignite a powerful cycle of development that fuels both individual and organizational excellence. By investing in continued professional growth, you not only empower your team to acquire valuable new skills, but you also cultivate a culture of high engagement, creativity, and productivity that drives the company forward.

When employees are engaged and confident, they are more satisfied in their jobs and less likely to leave your organization. In turn, your organization is more attractive to potential hires, allowing you to recruit more talented employees. When the newer employees start their professional growth path, the cycle begins again. Rinse and repeat.

Great companies don't just ALLOW their employees to grow; they EXPECT them to grow. They know that doing the same thing the same way over and over again will lead to stagnation with no advancement. In great, forward-thinking organizations, employees are measured by their desire to grow and their success in doing so. It is an important core value, something by which all are measured.

Managers often work to keep people "in their lane" because they believe it maintains efficiency and minimizes disruptions, which they perceive as crucial for meeting goals and deadlines. However, by not investing in and supporting employees' professional evolution, you risk inviting apathy toward their work or even pushing them out the door.

Peter Baeklund is credited with proposing this interaction, "A CFO asks a CEO: 'What happens if we invest in developing our people and then they leave us?' The CEO responds: 'What happens if we don't, and they stay?'"

If members of your team express an interest in learning or trying something, you must support them. It is also equally critical to find opportunities to push your team out of their comfort zone. By not only inspiring but also requiring growth, you show that you trust them, that you believe in them, and that you want them to try and fail and learn and try again. We all must take some risks in order to grow.

There are many small ways to encourage employees to grow. For instance, get feedback on a project from someone unexpected, like the receptionist or file clerk. Ask an assistant to sit in on a meeting and invite their input. Appoint someone to learn a new skill or software that can benefit the company and then report on it at a staff meeting. Give people a task that's out of their comfort zone. Inspire them to embrace it and to go a step further.

Go beyond just offering professional growth. Anticipate and champion it.

A Fire Has to Start with a Spark

With the advent of digital advertising and the proliferation of available media channels, the world of marketing has become more complex and dynamic than ever. Marketers who don't keep up get left behind.

A key emphasis at our advertising agency was hiring people who were smart, inquisitive, and thirsty for learning. We believed that our best employees were those who wanted to grow, and if they were motivated to develop their skills, they would be less likely to leave. This approach guided our hiring and management practices, fostering a culture of continuous improvement and professional development.

One member of our team, John, had strong potential but didn't seem to pursue the kind of ongoing education he needed to keep growing and achieve his potential. For two years, John had been doing the same job without looking at new ways of doing things. He seemed content with his routine, showing minimal interest in exploring new trends or techniques in the ever-evolving marketing landscape.

This was not the culture and learning environment we wanted in our workplace, and we knew we needed a way to spark John's skill set growth. Our goal was to help John grow as a professional, and in doing so, reinforce an environment where everyone felt encouraged to continually learn and improve.

John's breakthrough came when one of his colleagues, Lisa, got promoted over him to a more senior job with higher pay. Lisa had been with the company for a similar length of time but had consistently sought out new learning opportunities, attended industry conferences, and taken online courses to enhance her skills. Her promotion highlighted the value we placed on continuous professional growth.

John was not pleased that he'd been passed over. Lisa's promotion became a clear message to him and everyone on the team that the ongoing, self-motivated pursuit of professional growth was expected and would be rewarded.

Recognizing the opportunity to make this a Tiny Moment of realization for John, I scheduled a one-on-one meeting with him. During our conversation, I congratulated him on his solid performance but also gently pointed out the difference between his approach and Lisa's proactive learning attitude. I told him that, while we saw much value in his work, to move forward and take on more significant roles, it was essential that he keep growing and evolving. Lisa's promotion was a result of her continuous effort to learn and adapt to new challenges. I told him we wanted to support him in doing the same.

John seemed to take this to heart. He admitted that he had become comfortable in his current role and hadn't prioritized his professional development. We discussed setting specific goals for his development, including identifying areas where he could find relevant courses and workshops.

Following this conversation, it was evident that John had embraced this new approach. He began to watch industry webinars, enrolled in online courses, and started reading more about emerging trends. His renewed enthusiasm for learning was evident in his work, and he began contributing fresh ideas and strategies to the team.

John's transformation was a testament to the power of fostering a culture of continuous learning and growth, illustrating Bruce Springsteen's point that a spark is necessary to build a fire in "Dancing in the Dark." By taking a moment to provide constructive feedback and encouragement, we ignited his desire to evolve and improve. This Tiny Moment of leadership not only helped John realize his potential but also reinforced the importance of professional growth to the entire team.

CHAPTER FIFTY-ONE

Be Interested, Not Interesting

MANAGERS LECTURE. Leaders listen.

How you listen from your position as a leader sets a tone within your organization. Your listening permits others to listen as well. So, engage with curiosity and focus. Invite and stress the need for active participation in conversations, both big and small. Set high expectations for the engaged behavior of those around you.

> *When you make people feel important, they will act important.*

In his book *How to Win Friends and Influence People*, Dale Carnegie talked about the value of being interested. "If you want to be interesting," he suggests, "be interested."[1] When those around you feel that you are genuinely interested in them as individuals without an agenda and that you're listening for insight and not just waiting for your turn to speak, it allows them to feel safe and respected.

Be an active listener. Ask questions of your people. Solicit input. If you encourage those around you to think for themselves and give them the space to explore their own ideas, you will inspire gratitude that shows itself through commitment and loyalty.

Exceptional leaders encourage people to feel good about themselves and the organization. When you make people feel important, they will act important. This isn't about compliments, accolades, and applause, it's about respect. When you talk with people, set down your phone, notepad, and pen. Give them the focus you would want. Treat every conversation as if it's of the utmost importance because, in the long run, it is.

This idea is one of the simplest concepts in this book, but also one that many people forget—causing them to miss out on incredible opportunities.

It is essential for someone to feel like you're paying attention when they're talking to you. You don't want to be looking at your phone, glancing around, or interrupting with your own thoughts. You want to be engaged in what they're telling you.

Beyond that, you can truly demonstrate your interest by following up later. It's one thing to listen with interest as a coworker tells you about the play their daughter is going to be in over the weekend. It's something very different to circle back on Monday and say, "How did the play go over the weekend? Do you have a celebrity living in your house now?"

This small action can be especially effective for leaders because people know you are pulled in many directions through the course of a day with interruptions and demanding tasks to juggle. For you to prove that you care about the person and weren't just tolerating the conversation, let them know you were listening. The tiniest way to do this is by recalling the small things that people tell you after the fact.

"You mentioned this thing, and I came across this book and thought of you."

"Is your dog feeling better?"

"How is your knitting coming along?"

Celeste Headlee, in her outstanding TED Talk entitled "10 Ways to Have a Better Conversation," offers these tips for being a better listener:[2]

- "Don't multitask.

- Don't pontificate.

- Use open-ended questions.

- Go with the flow.

- If you don't know, say you don't know.

- Don't equate your experience with theirs.

- Don't repeat yourself.

- Stay out of the weeds.

- Listen.

- Be brief."

Headlee reminds us that being fully present and in the moment is the first step. She asks us to enter every conversation with the assumption that we have something to learn. "Conversations are not a promotional opportunity . . . talk should not be cheap." Assume that everybody you "meet knows something you don't."[3] Heed Buddha's wisdom: "If your mouth is open, you're not learning."

Everyone has something to teach us. "Most people do not listen with the intent to understand and learn; they listen with the intent to reply."[4] Let's be different. Let's be inspiring. In other words, let's be interested, not interesting.

It's easy to remember the exciting stuff, but it's more effective to remember and follow up on the mundane. That's a Tiny Moment any employee will genuinely appreciate.

A TINY MOMENT
Interest Pays Dividends

My kids grew up listening to my endless stream of quotes and sayings. I will admit I was hoping that if I wrapped up a lesson in a memorable phrase, they might hold on to it. I'd say it worked out reasonably well.

My daughter Kara often joined me in our team suite at hockey games, where we entertained key clients and their families. These events were full of conversation and networking. As a teenager, Kara understandably felt nervous when carrying on conversations with people she had never met.

One evening, she confided in me about her anxiety, telling me about her nervousness in those social situations. She told me she never knew what to say and was afraid people would find her boring.

"I think I have a solution," I said. "Try this. 'Be interested, not interesting.'"

She looked puzzled and asked what I meant. I explained that people love to talk about themselves and their experiences. When you show genuine interest in them, it makes them feel valued and appreciated. Kara didn't have to worry about being the most fascinating person in the room. Instead, she could focus on being a great listener and showing curiosity about others. Asking questions and listening to the answers would naturally make people find her engaging.

That Tiny Moment led to an important change in Kara's perspective. She absorbed the advice and began to put it into practice. At one game, I noticed Kara approaching a couple who were chatting by the buffet. I watched as she hesitated for a moment, then joined their conversation. Kara would tell me later that instead of worrying about what she should say, she started asking them questions like, "Are you enjoying the game? Do you have a favorite player? Where are you from?" As the couple responded to the questions, Kara listened and asked follow-up questions.

Kara continued this approach when she was with me at future hockey games. As the season progressed, she became more comfortable, and people found her more approachable and engaging. There was plenty to be interested in: families, jobs, hobbies. More than once, she came upon someone who shared her love of horses. Those were much longer conversations.

From that Tiny Moment on, Kara embraced the lesson of being interested rather than interesting. She continued to apply this principle in various social situations, whether it was at school, family gatherings, or other events. Years later, Kara told me that piece of advice changed everything for her. I smiled, knowing that the lesson had made a lasting impact on her life. It was a reminder that sometimes the simplest pieces of advice can have the most profound effects.

CHAPTER FIFTY-TWO

Deliver Plus One

I LOVE THE book *Raving Fans* by Ken Blanchard and Sheldon Bowles. It brilliantly uses a parable approach to teaching business and leadership skills. I have never forgotten the "deliver plus one" lesson it taught me.[1] The authors' advice:

As the lobby buzzed, I noticed a young boy, no older than seven or eight, standing off to the side in the concourse with tears streaming down his face.

First, decide what you want to be. What is your vision of your product or service? What is your "window" of what you can and will do for your customer?

Second, discover what the customer wants. Bring this together with your vision. You reveal the customer's vision in small bits, so your vision and their vision come together over time. Customers don't have complete visions. They are focused on two or three things and don't worry about the rest. Talk to your customers and learn what they want.

Finally, deliver plus one. When you offer something extra, people appreciate it. They feel like you are treating them as special and they're getting good value for their investment. The key is to add extras slowly, and only when you know all else is going well. When you overdeliver, don't overdo it. Go a little bit at a time. Sure, people always want more, but they most appreciate the self-initiated gesture you made in the first place.

This concept of exceeding expectations by just a little bit is extremely powerful. If you go too far, you run the risk of conditioning people to expect more rather than appreciate it. Imagine that a flight attendant comes down the aisle and offers you a second bag of peanuts. You might think, "Wow, nobody ever does that. That's nice." But what if they come and offer you twenty bags of peanuts? "Look, that's just too much. I get it, but you're trying too hard, and now it's ridiculous."

Eventually, as a culture of "plus one" takes hold, it becomes the accepted norm in the organization. Imagine if all our employees went a bit beyond the expected or required level of performance!

This approach doesn't focus on just meeting targets but also exceeding them. The "deliver plus one" maxim inspires employees to take initiative, be proactive, and consistently strive for excellence in their roles. By fostering this culture, leaders can cultivate a workforce that consistently goes the extra mile and delivers exceptional results.

When applied to our leadership style, this "plus one" concept can be powerful. Find a small, memorable way to elevate an employee's experience, offering enough to make a positive statement but only as much as makes sense. Grandiose gestures are planned and staged, but small, spontaneous "plus one" interactions can become meaningful Tiny Moments of great impact. Something as simple as, "How are your kids? You told me they were sick," can be that little something that you didn't have to say but did so as a way of going a bit beyond what was expected (and, as discussed in the last chapter, shows you are listening).

Grandiose moments may showcase a leader's ability to command attention, but smaller, more personal moments demonstrate authenticity and depth of connection.

In the realm of "deliver plus one," success is not a destination but a continuous journey. It's a commitment to consistently give more than you're expected to, setting the stage for exceptional achievements and leaving a remarkable impact. Teaching your employees this philosophy ensures that excellence becomes a way of life in which mediocrity has no place.

Inventor Charles Kettering said, "High achievement always takes place in the framework of high expectation." By consistently exceeding expectations and adding that extra touch of excellence, individuals and organizations can achieve not just success, but true distinction. It's a mindset that leaves a lasting impression by turning ordinary tasks into extraordinary results.

A TINY MOMENT
Little Gestures Make Big Impacts

When I was president of the Manchester Monarchs, one of my key roles was to be visible, approachable, and act as the face of the organization. As part of this, I made it a habit to stand in the lobby before every game, greeting fans as they arrived. I liked to see and be seen, ensuring that our supporters felt a direct connection to the organization.

On one particular game night, we had a special bobblehead giveaway. Our fans were excited as they lined up to receive their collectible. As the lobby buzzed, I noticed a young boy, no older than seven or eight, standing off to the side in the concourse with tears streaming down his face. Clutched in his tiny hands was an empty bobblehead box. He had lost his bobblehead and I watched him walk in disappointment with his family to their seats.

I spotted one of our newer employees, Nicole, nearby. She was always eager to learn and was enthusiastic about her role. I saw this as a perfect teaching moment. I approached Nicole and pointed out the distressed boy. "Nicole," I said, "this is an opportunity to make a real difference for one of our young fans."

I suggested she get another bobblehead from the lobby. She quickly returned with the replacement, and together we made our way down to the boy's seat in the arena. His parents were trying to console him, but he was clearly still quite upset.

I encouraged Nicole to take the lead. She knelt, held out the new bobblehead, and said, "I heard someone lost their bobblehead. Would you like this one?" The boy's face lit up with pure joy as he accepted the gift. His parents were equally appreciative, thanking Nicole profusely for the gesture.

Our gesture wasn't grandiose. It was actually quite simple. What was notable wasn't the magnitude of what we did; it was the fact that we did more than was expected and made a little boy very happy in the process.

Afterward, reinforcing the Tiny Moment we were sharing, I took Nicole aside and underlined the lesson behind our actions. I told Nicole that this is what it means to deliver plus one. It's not just about making up for a mistake or an unfortunate mishap; it's about creating moments that exceed expectations and leave lasting positive impressions.

Being visible and approachable isn't just a strategy; it's a commitment to our community and a promise to consistently "deliver plus one." This experience reinforced my belief in the power of going above and beyond for our fans. It served as a valuable lesson for Nicole on the impact of exceptional customer service.

CHAPTER FIFTY-THREE

Worst Idea Goes First

'M IN the advertising business, so I know a thing or two about ideas. It's what we do for a living.

Try starting an idea session by saying, "The worst idea goes first."

It can be intimidating for some to participate with a group of people tossing out ideas. Some may be worried about saying something out of fear of being laughed at or sounding "dumb." This is a shame, because great ideas generally come from an iterative process where various people in the group throw out all sorts of thoughts. Not all the ideas have to be award-winning, because no matter how "good" they are, these ideas stimulate and trigger other thoughts and ideas.

Scientist Linus Pauling said, "The best way to have a good idea is to have a lot of ideas." In a world where we are constantly being asked to come up with the perfect solution instantly, it can be very freeing not to have to come up with solutions and simply to have conversations.

There should be no penalty for bad ideas. No demerit points, no embarrassment, no shame. How much fun is that? You can freely say anything that comes to mind, knowing that the group will keep a little of one idea, a smidgen of another, and maybe throw another one out altogether. The point is that the group conversation and brainstorming bring out the best ideas. It's all additive, with each thought playing an important part in moving the process forward.

In Google's Project Aristotle study of 180 teams, "psychological safety" was ranked as the number one factor in team effectiveness and innovation. According to the study, "In a team with high psychological safety, teammates feel safe to take risks around their team members. They feel confident that no one on the team will embarrass or punish anyone else for admitting a mistake, asking a question, or offering a new idea."[1]

Depending on the organization, it can be challenging to create a safe place for new ideas, especially if the staff is not accustomed to being allowed to truly think freely and doesn't feel safe enough to blurt out anything that comes into their minds. The safer the environment, the greater the ideas that are created.

Here's an interesting approach. Try starting an idea session by saying, "The worst idea goes first." What a great way to take the pressure off and have some fun kicking off the discussion. With that as the opening introduction, who could possibly be nervous about throwing something out there, regardless of how unsure they are about it? If you're asking a team to come up with bad ideas, this might allow someone to suggest a crazy idea that they would otherwise fear suggesting. Once the bad ideas are on the table, some viable ideas may rise from the slush pile. At the very least, you've created an environment of open thinking.

I have long thought that everyone can be creative in their own way when allowed to be. Sure, some will have the reputation of being "wildly creative" and may come up with more than their share of great ideas. But everyone has a unique perspective and lens of their own, and it's amazing how much we can get out of the collective group when ALL feel free to contribute.

It's up to the leader to create a safe zone, encourage all ideas, and facilitate open thinking. Because the worst idea is no idea at all.

A TINY MOMENT
The More the Better

A few years ago, a hospital client at my ad agency wanted to run a campaign to emphasize their cutting-edge technology and forward-thinking approach to patient care. They wanted something that would position them as leaders in medical innovation. Our team was eager to tackle this challenge, knowing the importance of finding just the right words to encapsulate such a powerful message.

The creative team arrived at the brainstorming meeting excited and ready to work. Our creative director, Pete, kicked off the meeting by reminding everyone that we encourage the worst idea to go first. "So, let's hear all those crazy thoughts," he proclaimed.

For a moment, there was silence. Then, Brian, one of our more seasoned but quirky copywriters, raised his hand with a grin. "All right, here goes nothing. How about 'Hospital 2100: Into the Future'?"

The idea was indeed out there, sounding more suited to a sci-fi movie than a hospital ad campaign. Pete smiled and nodded as everyone in the room wrapped their heads around Brian's idea-starter. Pete thanked Brian for getting things started and then asked for other thoughts.

Chelsea was the first to build on Brian's offbeat suggestion. "I actually like the futuristic angle, but maybe we can tone it down." She continued by suggesting we focus on the concept of the future being accessible now, offering "Future Care, Today" as an idea.

Then Keith chimed in. "What about 'Tomorrow's Care, Today'?" He explained it was a bit more grounded while still conveying they are ahead of the curve.

As the room began buzzing with more energy, ideas bounced off the walls, each building upon the last. Brian's initial concept of "Hospital 2100: Into the Future" sparked a chain reaction of creativity.

Jake, our art director, added his twist on refining it further. "'Tomorrow's Care, Today' is close, but it could be even punchier. How about 'Next Is Now'?" He explained that it suggests that the hospital is at the cutting edge of what's happening right now, blending future advancements with present capabilities.

"Next Is Now" resonated with everyone in the room. It was concise yet powerful and perfectly captured the essence of what the hospital wanted to communicate.

We pitched the tagline "Next Is Now" to the hospital the following week. They were thrilled with how it conveyed their position as leaders in medical innovation and seamlessly combined the concepts of the future and the present. The tagline was approved on the spot.

Reflecting on that brainstorming session, I realized once again the power of our "Worst idea goes first" mantra. Brian's unpolished idea was the spark that ignited a creative process, leading to an excellent tagline. By creating a safe space for everyone to contribute, we unlocked our team's true potential, demonstrating that it's the willingness to embrace and explore the unconventional that often leads to the most extraordinary results.

CHAPTER FIFTY-FOUR

Encourage "Intrapreneurship"

NTREPRENEURS SEEK to discover opportunities where none previously existed. They convert new ideas and inventions into viable products. At its very core, entrepreneurship is an approach to solving real-world problems, often with breakthrough ideas, techniques, technology, or all three. Successful entrepre-

With an eye on market trends, intrapreneurs help their company stay ahead of the competition.

neurs are not driven by external stimuli, but from the inside. They do not wait for anything or anyone. Entrepreneurship is synonymous with passion.

As the great Diana Ross said, "You can't just sit there and wait for people to give you that golden dream. You've got to get out there and make it happen for yourself."

Entrepreneurs make it happen for themselves.

A study conducted at the Enterprise Research Centre in the UK cited challenge, independence, and recognition as the primary motivations for entrepreneurs to strike out on their own. They typically value innovation, autonomy, and the challenge of problem-solving. The opportunity to create something new, control their destiny, and experience personal growth are key drivers. Ultimately, entrepreneurs are passionate about their ideas and find fulfillment in building businesses that contribute to their sense of achievement.[1]

But to act on their ideas, entrepreneurs must leave the comfort and certainty of a fixed job and a steady paycheck for the thrill of building something new. As a result, the act of entrepreneurship is fraught with risk.

Wouldn't it be great if this entrepreneurial spirit were celebrated, supported, and rewarded within the company without great risk to the individual? There's no financial ruin as there would be if they started a business on their own and failed. Instead, there would be internal recognition and reward for their ideas, or a hard, but valuable, lesson learned by failing.

Say hello to intrapreneurs. Intrapreneurs are the self-motivated, proactive people who bring fresh ideas to life within an organization. They're the ones who see a challenge and find creative solutions that boost productivity or save money. With an eye on market trends, intrapreneurs help their company stay ahead of the competition. They're the spark that drives innovation and growth, playing a key role in shaping the company's future.

Employers need to recognize and reward valuable intrapreneurs to keep them. Intrapreneurs who are not recognized and rewarded will likely leave for another company or perhaps go out on their own. However, when a leader allows people to think and behave like entrepreneurs within the walls of a bigger organization, this "intrapreneurship" builds confidence in the employees and sets the foundation to discover new opportunities.

One of the most well-known examples is the story of how Post-it notes were invented. In the early 1970s, 3M scientist Art Fry was searching for a bookmark that would neither fall out nor damage his church hymnal. Fry noticed that a scientist colleague at 3M, Spencer Silver, PhD, had developed an adhesive that was strong enough to stick to surfaces and could be repositioned or removed without leaving residue. Fry took some of Silver's adhesive and applied it along the edge of a piece of paper. He solved his church hymnal problem! Fry and Silver soon realized that this "bookmark" had other potential functions. They used one to leave a note on a work file, and coworkers kept dropping by, seeking "bookmarks" for their offices. This "bookmark" was a new way to communicate and organize. 3M Corporation crafted the name Post-it note for Fry's bookmarks and began production in the late '70s for commercial use.

The rest is history, all sparked by Silver's ability to think and work independently within the company. What would a world without Post-it notes even be like?

A TINY MOMENT
Let Employees Help Drive Change

When I worked for the Philadelphia Phillies, one of my responsibilities was heading up the group that operated our computerized ticketing system, a system that was advanced for its time. We had streamlined the ticketing process, ensuring fans could easily purchase tickets and enjoy their experience at the ballpark. Despite its effectiveness, the system was somewhat expensive to maintain and operate.

During an annual budget meeting with my boss, David, I voiced my concerns. "David, I'm really worried about how much our ticketing system is costing us," I said. "We're running an efficient operation, but expenses keep going up."

David leaned back in his chair and in one extraordinary Tiny Moment, said something that would change the course of my career. "Maybe we could offer our ticketing services to some of the other sports organizations in town. If they pay us to use our system, we could defray some of these costs."

That personal conversation and his in-the-moment suggestion sparked an intrapreneurial spirit within me. I was always focused on optimizing our internal processes, but this idea opened my eyes to a new realm of possibilities. The concept of leveraging our expertise to generate additional revenue was an exciting proposition for me.

Over the next few weeks, I began exploring how we could market our ticketing system to other sports teams in Philadelphia. I reached out to some of my contacts in the Philadelphia area, finding each conversation to be a learning experience. The more I delved into it, the more I realized the potential of David's suggestion.

My first "pitch" meeting was with the Philadelphia 76ers, and I remember it vividly. As I outlined how our system could enhance their ticketing operations, their CFO leaned forward and said, "I want to explore this with some others here, Jeff. This really does have the potential to improve our ticket operations." When I heard this, I realized that we were onto something.

Within two years, we had successfully onboarded the 76ers, the Philadelphia Eagles, and Temple University onto our ticketing system. These organizations paid us fees that significantly defrayed the cost of our operations. The success of this venture not only eased our budget concerns but also positioned the Phillies as a leader in innovative solutions within both the region and the sports industry.

This journey taught me the power of innovative thinking within an organization. With the right mindset and a Tiny Moment or two from leadership, employees can drive significant change and create new value, not just for their team but for the entire organization. Intrapreneurship can thrive when leaders encourage their teams to think beyond their immediate responsibilities. Sometimes, the best ideas come from looking at our challenges from a different angle and finding ways to turn them into opportunities.

CHAPTER FIFTY-FIVE

You're on Stage. Always.

LEADERS ARE never out of the spotlight. They are always on stage. There's a time and place to submerge yourself in thinking about the big picture, the what-ifs and the to-dos. But it's not

People draw strength from leaders who appear in control, especially during turbulent times.

when you're face-to-face with your team, who are there to bond, work together, and succeed. They are looking for a confident face of positivity and encouragement. As Paul Boyles once said, "Leaders are always on stage. Everyone is watching what you do or don't do—always."[1]

People are innately curious about leaders because they have such an important and pervasive impact on the ongoing flow and success of the business. Many leaders have the charisma that demands attention even when just walking through an office. Maintaining the right demeanor at the right moment, especially when in the public eye, is a crucial aspect of leadership. One of the ways workers will gauge how things are going is not only by listening to their leaders but also by observing their body language.

Do not waste this opportunity by expressing an emotion that is not right for the moment. Understand the impact of your demeanor when you're visible. A stormy one can change the temperature of the room very quickly. But it's not enough to just refrain from looking negative; you must leverage the opportunity of the moment by being positive and upbeat. This will have a huge positive impact on your people's mood and energy. The legendary management consultant Peter Drucker once noted, "Your body language, expressions and overall presence communicate volumes to your team."[2]

A serious and stoic presence might just be an innocent byproduct of an active mind, but it is still one to be conscious of because it can easily be misinterpreted as a negative vibe by those you are leading.

The phrase "never let them see you sweat" was popularized as a slogan in the 1980s by a series of advertisements for Gillette's antiperspirant products. The campaign aimed to highlight the effectiveness of their antiperspirants by suggesting that even in challenging situations, the product would help individuals remain sweat-free and confident. This concept wasn't new to leadership. We have long known that when leaders remain composed and self-assured, their ability to maintain emotional stability under pressure becomes apparent, leading people to trust them as a resolute and authoritative figure.

By combining the awareness that "you're always on stage" with the commitment to "never let them see you sweat," you can project a confident leadership presence that makes everyone around you feel more confident. When leaders exude confidence and poise, they set a tone of stability and reliability. People draw strength from leaders who appear in control, especially during turbulent times. This inspiration often comes not just from the words a leader speaks but from the demeanor they carry.

Leaders must recognize the power of their presence and the profound impact it has on those around them. By consciously projecting positivity, remaining composed under pressure, and understanding the significance of their "on stage" moments, leaders can foster an environment of confidence and motivation.

A TINY MOMENT
They'll Be Watching You

Tiny Moments can come from unexpected sources, as I learned firsthand when a fan at a hockey game reminded me that, as the president of the hockey team, I was always on stage. During my days in sports, I was known for mingling with the fans. This helped me meet more of them, stay plugged in to the experience, and maintain a strong connection with the community.

While walking around the stadium or arena, I often found myself deep in thought, contemplating a situation I had observed, a recent conversation, or maybe an operational issue. In these moments, I wouldn't realize that my deep contemplation translated into a distant appearance, often with furrowed brows and tight lips. I felt fine, but my deep contemplation caused my facial expression to look distant and perhaps worried.

One time, a fan in the concourse saw me in this state and thought something was wrong. In what would become a Tiny Moment that I remember to this day, the fan asked, "Jeff, are you okay?"

To an outsider, it could appear that I was upset or even angry when, in fact, my thoughts were centered on exciting and interesting challenges. But at a sporting event, where people come to have fun, I appeared somber and unsmiling. Not a good look!

This Tiny Moment encounter made me acutely aware of the importance of one's outward expression. I learned to be mindful of what I was thinking about in the context of my surrounding environment. As a leader, people are always watching you, whether they are fans in an arena or employees in a workplace. Your demeanor can significantly impact their perception and experience.

From then on, when I was out with fans, I began to see it as my stage. I understood the importance of displaying the persona my audience expected when they paid money and showed up to have fun. I made it a point to smile, talk, and joke with them, always ensuring my visual expression sent a positive message. The myriad of things on my mind at any one time had to remain "behind the curtain."

As my career evolved, this lesson extended beyond my interactions with fans. At my agency, I am always aware that employees, much like fans, are keenly observant of their leaders. They take cues from our behavior and attitudes, which can influence their morale and productivity.

By maintaining a positive outward expression, I fostered a more engaging and supportive environment, both in the arena and in the office. This practice helped reinforce the importance of approachability and positivity in leadership, reminding me that, as a leader, I am always on stage.

CHAPTER FIFTY-SIX

Take the Bullet

'LL PUT it bluntly—mistakes suck. They interrupt momentum and can be a blow to the ego, personally and professionally, individually and companywide. They happen, and we hate them. Admitting we've made them can be painful, awkward, and demeaning.

It takes a village for one misstep or error in judgment to turn into a real problem, and that village has one person in charge of the ultimate results—you.

This is consistent with the importance of failure we discussed earlier in the book when talking about FAILing forward. It remains true that failing is necessary to gain new understanding and learn from it. What becomes so important is having a positive, safe environment to deal with these situations so we can turn a negative into something positive.

In many ways, good leadership is defined more by challenges than successes. A culture of owning errors with honesty and dignity sets a positive stage for your team—and this starts with you. When it comes to team setbacks, it can be easy to finger-point and blame others. And blame can result in demotivation, tension, and resentment that affects productivity and engagement.

Interestingly, a University of Illinois Urbana-Champaign study found that people think it's inappropriate to shift blame and don't have respect for people who do it.[1] Still, they expect corporate leaders to shift the blame. Leaders need to change that low expectation.

Everyone must be accountable but rarely does the responsibility lie with one person. It takes a village for one misstep or error in judgment to turn into a real problem, and that village has one person in charge of the ultimate results—you.

Success should, of course, always be shared by the team and reflect positively on the leader. However, if you are in a formal leadership role, you are also ultimately responsible when things go wrong. It may not be obvious that a specific error falls to a specific person, but a good leader doesn't throw anyone under the bus to minimize their involvement in the problem. They accept responsibility on behalf of the team, develop solutions, and welcome feedback.

Businessman Arnold H. Glasgow put it this way: "A good leader takes a little more than his share of the blame, a little less than his share of the credit."[2]

While leaders accept and demand accountability, you must lead by example to inspire people to accept responsibility. This starts with sharing the successes with the team AND owning the mistakes along with the staff. And they always look for learning (and teaching) opportunities.

If the captain steers the ship into shark-infested waters and doesn't help the crew learn how to navigate those waters, then it's not the fault of the crew that they're in trouble. Likewise, the captain cannot be solely responsible for returning the ship to safety.

Leaders must remember that they are ultimately responsible for the actions of their employees. Was someone asked to handle a project and make decisions for which they weren't prepared? If yes, that's ultimately the indiscretion of either the top leader or someone who reports to them in the chain. So, take your share of the responsibility and ensure that others understand their role in the situation. The fact that you step up to face this scrutiny together is the important thing, and that gesture speaks volumes. People can accept the need to improve when they feel they are not alone and targeted. They want to know you have their back in a fair way.

Taking responsibility for the team doesn't necessarily mean taking on every burden and problem the team faces. Acknowledging your role as the leader, apologizing for any missteps, and owning the situation with those involved are important and appreciated. Still, it's equally important, if not more so, to move on with solutions. In doing so, don't make the mistake of allowing those you lead to push every responsibility upward. If there isn't an obvious fix, ask for guidance and feedback on how to make things right.

Mistakes happen. Let's reduce them with good training, attentive oversight, and smart assignment of duties. But let's understand the power of our response as leaders and ensure we respond in a way that builds our organization rather than creates resentment and leads to poor future performance.

Take responsibility for your actions and those of your group.

A TINY MOMENT
Don't Play the Blame Game

As a leader in the sports industry, I was always prepared to take responsibility for issues that arose on my watch. However, when a difficult fan named Chet exploded on the other end of the line, I knew that this situation would be particularly challenging to manage.

Chet had been a season ticket holder for years. Unfortunately, Jim, one of our new sales reps, made a mistake when he inadvertently sold Chet's seats to another customer. Chet was both passionate and well-connected. If we couldn't come up with an effective solution for him and the new customer, it would be problematic.

Jim was understandably nervous about the situation that he had caused, and he dreaded the fallout. I pulled him aside and after reviewing what had gone wrong, I told him that I would call Chet and work things out. The relief on Jim's face was noticeable. In this one Tiny Moment of learning, I demonstrated the importance of leaders taking responsibility and ownership for mistakes, even if they didn't cause them. It was a lesson that would benefit Jim for years to come.

I was prepared for the worst when I called Chet, and that's what I got. He began yelling before I even had a chance to speak. "I can't believe that you guys would treat me like this! I've been a loyal customer for years, and now you've gone and given away my seats!" I listened, understanding where he was coming from, and made sure that his complaints were heard. When he finally ran out of steam, I told him that I was responsible for the mistake and that I would make it right.

The solution we worked out was reasonable. All we had to do was move Chet over one seat, and both customers would be well served. I offered him other options as well, including upgraded seats in a better section for no additional charge. I told him that I would meet him in person to show him all the options we had for him. It was an approach that would take up a lot of time on my end, but I knew it was necessary. When I met with Chet the following week, I quickly apologized again, and he thanked me for taking ownership of the situation. We proceeded to resolve the issue to his satisfaction.

Even though I had not made the mistake personally, my employee had, and I knew it was my responsibility to "take the bullet" for the situation. I was much better equipped to handle it than Jim would have been. Doing so let Chet know that we were committed to owning up to our mistakes, and also made a big statement to Jim, who would feel more than ever that management had his back.

As a leader, I knew that the sports business is one of relationships, and connections like Chet's are what make it thrive. The reputation of a business in this industry can have a significant impact, and I knew that if Chet felt like he'd been taken care of, he would likely speak about it positively with his friends, family, and colleagues.

As a leader, you must be prepared to take the heat, even for situations that may not be entirely your fault. When taking accountability, it shows both customers and employees that you are more committed to finding the right solution than placing blame.

CHAPTER FIFTY-SEVEN

Sacrifice Raises the Level
of Commitment

THE FILM *Office Space* brilliantly
highlights the clear difference between
managers and leaders.[1] For many
people, Bill Lumbergh (played by Gary Cole)
telling Rob Livingston's Peter that he needs
him to come in on a Saturday hit painfully
close to home, as it was clear that Bill was
expecting sacrifices from the team that he
wasn't planning to make himself.

Leadership is not about personal gain, but about making sacrifices for the team's success.

The best way to get people to pursue a vision is for the leader to sacrifice
alongside them willingly. Leaders need to consider the personal cost before
they ask others to join them, with the "joining" being a key component. If
a team feels that a leader is asking them to make all the sacrifices while the
manager kicks back and reaps all the credit and rewards, they won't stick
around for long. Imagine the leader is in the trenches with them, doing the
work, missing a personal function or two, and acknowledging the sacrifices
made by everyone. In that case, it will feel less lonely and thankless, even
if the demands are no easier.

Leaders need to deliver the "we're in this together" message and then prove
it by showing up and buckling down to earn respect and gain buy-in.

Leadership is not about personal gain, but about making sacrifices for the team's success. The life of a leader can look glamorous, but the reality is that leadership requires sacrifices. As John Maxwell said, "A leader must give up to go up."[2]

As you rise in leadership, responsibilities increase and, in certain ways, rights decrease. When leaders accept their job, they accept the responsibility and accountability that go with it. That means that they must be willing to give up more than the people they lead. Leadership means sacrifice, and the higher the leadership level, the greater the sacrifice.

If it's impossible for you as the leader to be side by side through the challenging work, you can make other sacrifices to show support for the work that needs to be done. Pay for meals, grant extra time off, and give out gifts to acknowledge work well done. This demonstrates that while you were not able to be integrally involved this time, you still recognize and appreciate the efforts of others.

Ralph Waldo Emerson observed, "For everything you have missed, you have gained something else and for everything you gain, you lose something."[3] Leaders would do well to embrace this perspective, recognizing that generous sacrifice often leads to success in many forms.

A TINY MOMENT
Take One for the Team

I was working for the Milwaukee Brewers, leading a staff of over twenty-five people in the ticket sales and marketing department. Our team was to represent the Brewers at a community event, make connections, and collect sales leads. Four representatives would be required to cover the responsibilities we had planned. However, the night before the event, I received a call from one of the people scheduled to participate in the event. She told me she had a stomach virus and would not be able to attend.

I called Trea, the senior member of the assigned group, to discuss our dilemma. Trea spent the next two hours calling other staff members, but he was not able to find anyone who was available. I could sense the stress in Trea's voice as he explained that three people would struggle to manage the event effectively.

At that moment, even though I had plans that would need to change, I knew as the leader it was vital for me to step up and join them. Not only would my presence help make the event successful, but it would also demonstrate to my staff that I was willing to sacrifice for the good of the team.

The next day, as we arrived at the venue, I could see the relief on Trea's face and the gratitude in the eyes of the other team members. They knew I had rearranged my schedule to be there. Throughout the day, we worked together seamlessly to ensure that everything ran smoothly. My willingness to join them in the trenches created a palpable sense of unity and commitment within the team.

In those few hours, a subtle yet powerful transformation took place. The team's commitment deepened, and their respect for me as a leader grew. They realized that I valued their efforts and was willing to make sacrifices for our collective success. This Tiny Moment, which may seem insignificant to an outsider, reinforced the bond within our group and set a standard for what true leadership meant. My gesture of solidarity inspired them to raise their game and match my level of dedication.

By the end of the day, we had not only successfully managed the event but had also strengthened our team spirit. My decision to join them paid off in ways that went beyond immediate results. It showed that leadership is not just about making decisions from a position of authority but also about being willing to make personal sacrifices for the good of the team. It is these moments of sacrifice that elevate everyone's commitment and create a culture of mutual respect and dedication.

CHAPTER FIFTY-EIGHT

Welcome the Messenger of Conflict

I ADMIT THAT I like to debate. Note that I didn't say "argue." That's different.

My concept of debate is active minds having a healthy back-and-forth discussion about various thoughts, ideas, and approaches to arrive at the best possible

Debate makes us better, but only if we don't take things personally.

solution(s) to a given project or issue. Debate strives to use facts, draw out healthy discussion, consider various perspectives, vet different mindsets, and move an undertaking toward its best outcome. It is indeed not about what you say but more so how gracefully and respectfully you say it.

An argument is merely an emotion-driven (sometimes ego-driven) quarrel. It's not at all the same as a healthy debate. Quite often, when you're fighting with someone, you don't truly comprehend the other side of the story because you're too busy not listening to be open to it.

In this book, we've talked a lot about the safe, free flow of ideas, productive collaboration, and giving everyone a voice. The best way to accomplish this—I dare say the only way—is to encourage as much spirited conversation as possible and consider anything the group can reasonably imagine. How can we possibly be our best without encouraging and considering a myriad of diverse ideas and concepts?

"Groupthink" of similar ideas presented by like-minded people yields a mediocre result. A robust dialogue and deliberation of a wide variety of ideas, often in conflict with each other, always arrive at a better place.

"Conflict" is a strong word, but it doesn't have to be negative. Conflict can be positive and healthy when we challenge each other respectfully, are open to contrary ideas, and collaborate candidly. (Remember how we talked about carefrontation in chapter 22.) The most effective teams are those where people feel safe to disagree and challenge each other. No one person has all the answers. Keeping disagreements and the environment positive builds trust as issues are worked through together. This is not the time to take things personally, but rather understand that this is strictly about business.

As John Wooden said, "Whatever you do in life, surround yourself with smart people who'll argue with you." (Apparently, Mr. Wooden doesn't mind using the word "argue." I'll stick with "debate," but the point is the same.)

I served on the board of the Center for Ethics at Saint Anselm College in Manchester, New Hampshire, for many years. The Center draws upon five guiding principles to foster solutions for the common good. These principles help guide us through disagreement, ensuring that even in conflict, we can work toward understanding and positive outcomes. These are the five guiding principles:

- Reflection

- Communication

- Listening

- Empathy

- Deliberation

Having differing opinions and perspectives about things is not a bad thing. As we discussed previously, there are indispensable benefits derived from "disagreement." Things only turn bad if we do not accept our differences as positive and embrace the opportunity that this offers to develop a better thought process, better understanding, and, ultimately, better solutions. Following the principles of the Center for Ethics, or any other approach to collaboration, allows for the healthiest and most rewarding environment.

In business, as in life, there will be struggles and challenges that need to be faced. A genuine "get-along" culture is one of debate, because if we want to truly get along, we must talk to each other openly and honestly. The cultures that get along are the ones that can respectfully discuss what's on their mind, hash things out respectfully, and move on to do great things together.

As the song "Metal & Dust" by the band London Grammar astutely observes, arguing is not the same as fighting, which is an interesting way to think about how we can express our disagreement with someone. Again, the word "argue" can be loaded for many; let's go with our word: "We debate, we don't fight."

Managers might hope for a "get-along culture," but great leaders invite, inspire, and even instigate debate. They know that debate makes us better, but only if we don't take things personally. The sweet spot is a culture in which conflicts are played out in the open, but everyone is focused on the group being right rather than proving themselves right, and a culture in which disagreement is a challenge to be met rather than a threat to be repelled. It makes us smarter, and, counterintuitively, when done well, it brings us closer together.

In the words of author Frank Sonnenberg, "How will you know if your ideas are sound if you don't let people challenge them?"[1]

A TINY MOMENT
Embracing the Disruptor

We were working on a new campaign at the ad agency, and since I was very involved with this client, I had ideas about how we would approach the campaign. I was confident that my insights aligned with the client's perspective. When I presented my ideas to the group, the response was very positive. There were nods in agreement and enthusiasm for the direction we were heading.

However, amid this collective approval, Gerry raised his hand. Gerry often had different ideas and was known for challenging the status quo, sometimes causing friction within the team. As he began to speak, I noticed a few colleagues rolling their eyes, anticipating another disruption.

I am a firm believer in the principle of "welcoming the messenger of conflict" and believe it's crucial to listen to dissenting voices, as they can offer valuable perspectives that might otherwise be overlooked. In a Tiny Moment that led the group to better understand the value of contrasting views, I asked Gerry to continue and fully express his thoughts. He proposed a completely different approach, one that diverged significantly from what we had been discussing. His ideas were bold and unconventional, and while not all of them were immediately applicable, there were several points that made us pause and reconsider our initial plan.

Gerry's ideas inspired us to re-evaluate our assumptions and think critically about our strategy. His perspective highlighted some potential weaknesses in our approach that we hadn't considered. For example, he pointed out that our initial plan was heavily focused on digital media, which, while important, might not resonate as well with a segment of the client's target audience that still engaged with traditional media channels. Gerry's suggestion to incorporate a more integrated media strategy, blending digital with traditional elements, sparked a lively discussion among the team.

As we debated and dissected Gerry's points, it became clear that while his approach required more effort and resources, it had the potential to create a more comprehensive and effective campaign. His willingness to challenge consensus pushed us out of our comfort zones and encouraged us to explore new ideas.

In the end, we synthesized the best aspects of both approaches. We retained the core elements of my initial plan, which provided a solid foundation, and integrated Gerry's suggestions to enhance the campaign's reach and impact. The final campaign was a hybrid of tested strategies and fresh creative concepts, resulting in a more robust and versatile solution.

The experience reaffirmed my belief in the importance of fostering an environment where diverse opinions are not only tolerated but encouraged. By welcoming conflict and embracing different perspectives, we can achieve greater innovation and effectiveness. Gerry's willingness to challenge the group and our openness to his ideas ultimately led us to a better solution.

This episode also underscored the value of listening and collaboration within a team. It's easy to become complacent and stick with ideas that receive unanimous approval, but actual growth and improvement often come from questioning and refining those ideas. As a leader, it was my responsibility to ensure that I hear every voice and that we remain open to new and challenging viewpoints, just like Gerry's, even though they may initially feel like conflict.

CHAPTER FIFTY-NINE

No Data Without Story, No Story Without Data

THERE'S NOTHING sexy about data to most people. It's facts and figures, spreadsheets and math. But it's also a powerful tool for validation, affirmation, and even inspiration. It's one

Look for the story in the data. Dig for the data in the story.

thing to make a point or persuade someone to see things your way. You share your perspective and convince them that your point of view is not off base. Your story might be compelling, but without the backing of solid data, persuading and inspiring might be an uphill battle.

If you have real facts in the form of data to underscore the "why," your argument takes on authoritative weight.

Data is science. It's based on facts and it's not emotional. If the story is the what, the data is the why. These two things are interconnected and interdependent. Data without a story is hollow. A story without the data is just a daydream. No one cared that someone looked up at the moon and wondered if we might be able to fly there someday until someone else applied data and science to that fantasy.

Establishing and communicating measurement systems removes the guesswork and introduces data points for strategy and accountability. Invite everyone to test and measure these data and measurement systems to make better decisions and avoid mishaps. These tests don't need to be complicated; hard tests, fast tests, partial tests—they are all helpful and important.

In our daily work, we constantly juggle between the data and the story. We present an idea and then the facts are sought to support or reject that idea. Sometimes the data for one thing inspires an idea for something else. Sometimes a client will bring us a question, and we use the data to support our reply, or we might take a client a bold idea that they scoff at until the data proves the concept worthy of consideration.

A simple yet transformative change leaders can make is to consistently incorporate brief, compelling anecdotes or narratives when presenting data. This practice bridges the gap between the analytical nature of data and the human element of storytelling. For instance, when sharing a set of data points, a leader could frame it within a real-world scenario or personal experience. This brief story could recount how the data was collected, the challenges faced, or the impact it had on a specific individual or team.

Leaders find a way to balance this teeter-totter between data and story. Throughout the day, or even a single conversation, more weight may be given to either side for a bit, but the scale never fully tips to one side. When you are too focused on the story or data, reposition the discussion from the other side. Look for the story in the data. Dig for the data in the story. Any good plan of action will always include both.

A TINY MOMENT
Data with a Soul

Data-driven decisions are the backbone of successful advertising campaigns. However, an often-overlooked element is the narrative that makes sense of the data, giving it life and relevance. This truth became crystal clear to me years ago when we were working on a campaign for a senior living brand looking to promote their independent living options. The data we gathered was impressive. We had detailed demographics, psychographics, and social media insights. Our analysts had parsed mountains of information, producing charts and graphs that highlighted key trends and consumer behaviors. On paper, everything looked perfect.

When we presented the data to the client, the initial reaction was positive. They appreciated the depth of our analysis and the precision of our targeting. However, as the meeting progressed, I noticed a lack of genuine excitement or engagement. The client nodded along, but there was no spark, no connection to the wealth of information laid out before them.

After the meeting, I realized we had fallen into a common trap. We had data, but we lacked a compelling story to tie it all together. The data alone, while accurate and thorough, wasn't enough to inspire action. It was a humbling realization that despite our expertise and hard work, we were missing a crucial element. This Tiny Moment profoundly impacted my approach to leadership. It reinforced the importance of balance and integration, teaching me to value both analytical precision and creative storytelling.

Determined to turn things around with the client, I gathered my team for a brainstorming session. I emphasized the importance of narrative and how we needed to weave a story that resonated with the client's vision and objectives. We needed to transform the data from static numbers into a dynamic, relatable story that would captivate and engage.

One of our junior team members, Mia, came up with a great idea. She suggested that we focus on a single, compelling persona who embodied the target demographic. Our profile described Martha, a vibrant seventy-five-year-old who is still quite active. Mia proposed we build our narrative around Martha's journey, illustrating how our client's independent living community integrated perfectly with her stage in life.

As we fleshed out Martha's story, we used the data to support every aspect of her experience. The statistics on senior consumer behavior, the impact of family in the decision, and optimal geographic targeting all found a place in our narrative. We didn't discard the data, but instead, we gave it context and meaning through Martha's story.

Brené Brown once said, "Maybe stories are just data with a soul."[1] And that's what we gave the client. When we presented the revised campaign to the client, the difference was profound. This time, their eyes lit up as we introduced them to Martha and took them through a day in her life. The data that had previously seemed dry and impersonal now came alive, illustrating a clear, relatable path to success. The client was not only engaged but also genuinely excited about the campaign's potential.

This Tiny Moment of learning—realizing the necessity of pairing data with a compelling story—became a cornerstone of our agency's approach. The principle of "No Data Without Story, No Story Without Data" became a mantra within our team. We learned to view data and narrative as two sides of the same coin, each essential to creating campaigns that resonate deeply with our clients and their audiences.

CHAPTER SIXTY

Protect Your Informants

A S A leader, you know a lot of what is going on. Yet there's also a lot that you don't know.

Leaders can't know everything (or want to, for that matter). Yes, you want to know the most important things to the business, but not so much that all the little things start to cloud significant issues.

> *Nothing destroys trust faster than broken confidentiality.*

However, some things going on underneath the surface are helpful and important to know. You don't need to overreact and jump into action on every little piece of news, but the more you know about what's going on, the better you can decide which elements are important enough for you to address and which are not.

Sometimes, little things can grow into big things. The art becomes distinguishing between the non-essential things you can ignore and the issues that may seem small but should be addressed so they don't bubble up to be more troublesome or disruptive.

The first step is to put yourself in a position to be aware of what is going on under the radar in the organization. You can create and foster this flow of organizational intelligence by establishing a trusted channel of information to the top without the fear of exposure and reprisal.

As a leader, you have a variety of sources of information. Some are standard, such as sales reports, written documentation, and final work submissions. However, access to other sources or tidbits of information can be less direct and available. Perhaps someone is aware of an unhappy coworker or unsatisfied client. If this person feels the information is not theirs to share, they may be nervous about being exposed as an informant.

The most challenging aspect of cultivating the trust necessary for this flow of information is protecting your source. Responding too hastily without taking care to protect the source can stifle the future flow of such information and it can cause conflict between teammates.

With the unhappy coworker, you could schedule one-on-ones with everyone on the team so that it doesn't appear direct and personal to one individual. And it's certainly feasible to check on a client's happiness with your work out of genuine curiosity. It doesn't need to indicate any insider information was shared.

Learning to work with your informants can be challenging because they may feel insecure about bringing you a grievance. They may fear they are overreacting or will be seen as sensitive or a "tattletale" if others should find out. More than anything, make them feel safe and secure in telling you. You must never betray the sanctity of a personal conversation originally founded in trust.

Nothing destroys trust faster than broken confidentiality. It speaks to credibility and character, and it's nearly impossible to fix once it's tarnished. Protect your team's chemistry by respecting the information that is shared with you and utilizing it with care. Great leaders know how to leverage insight for the good of the team and company.

A TINY MOMENT
The Tightrope of Confidentiality

I have always prided myself on fostering a transparent and open environment, believing in the power of honest communication. However, one incident early in my career as a leader stands out as a lesson in the delicate balance between transparency and confidentiality—a lesson learned the hard way.

One afternoon, during a routine check-in with my team, I received a private message from Lisa, one of our junior staff members. She hesitated at first but then confided in me about a troubling issue: Tom, a senior staff member, had been taking credit for ideas that weren't his. According to Lisa, this had happened multiple times, and it was starting to affect the morale and motivation of the junior staff. Lisa felt compelled to speak up because she believed it was hurting our collaborative culture.

Lisa's news surprised me. Tom was a respected and influential figure in the organization, known for his strong leadership and creativity. Nonetheless, I knew I had to address the issue promptly. Fueled by a sense of urgency and a desire to uphold our values, I decided to confront Tom directly.

But in my eagerness to resolve the situation, I made a grave mistake. During the meeting with Tom, I revealed that Lisa had brought the issue to my attention. Tom's demeanor changed instantly—his shock quickly turned to defensiveness, and he vehemently denied the accusations. He felt betrayed and singled out, and his trust in both Lisa and me was shattered.

The fallout was severe. Word quickly spread throughout the office about the confrontation, and soon, the entire team was aware of the situation. Lisa's colleagues distanced themselves from her, fearing that she could also expose their grievances. Tom, feeling resentful, began to distance himself from both Lisa and the team, his once vibrant leadership now replaced with a cold, detached approach.

The team's chemistry deteriorated. The incident damaged the open, collaborative environment we had worked so hard to build. Trust, the very foundation of our teamwork, was eroded, and it became clear that repairing these relationships would be a long and arduous process.

In a Tiny Moment of enlightenment, I realized that in my zeal to address the issue, I had overlooked the importance of confidentiality and the potential repercussions of revealing my source. This misjudgment caused a ripple effect that undermined our entire team dynamic.

To rebuild trust, I had to take full responsibility for my actions. I called a team meeting and openly acknowledged my mistake, apologizing for my breach of confidence to Tom and Lisa specifically and then to the entire team. I then implemented new policies to ensure such a breach would not happen again, emphasizing the importance of handling sensitive information with the utmost discretion.

Rebuilding the team's trust took time and effort. To restore the sense of safety and mutual respect, we held team-building exercises, open forums for airing grievances anonymously, and one-on-one check-ins. Gradually, the team began to heal, but the scars of that incident served as a constant reminder of the importance of handling delicate information with care.

This experience profoundly shaped my approach to leadership. It taught me the critical importance of balancing transparency with confidentiality and the potential damage that can result from mishandling sensitive information.

Act like a reporter: Never reveal your sources. While honesty and openness are vital, so too is the responsibility to protect the trust and integrity of the team. It was a painful lesson but one that ultimately made me a more thoughtful and cautious leader.

CHAPTER SIXTY-ONE

Never Waste a Crisis

WE ALL have problems. They are an inevitable part of life. The question is not if but when the next "issue" will arise and what its magnitude will be.

There are the smaller problems—the annoyances and inconveniences that really aren't a big deal but just irk you a little bit. They fit into a "there's always something" category and they don't amount to much in the end.

The phrase "never waste a crisis" means taking advantage of a challenging situation as an opportunity for positive change or growth.

Then there are the bigger ones. The kind that really get your attention. These are the problems that genuinely do make waves and cause disruption. Performance issues or departures among senior staff members. Losing a big client. Fundamental market shifts and corrections out of your control. These are not small, inconsequential developments. And if not handled well, these can increase stress, create conflict, weaken productivity, and ultimately decrease revenue.

But remember what I said earlier in the book: True character reveals itself in times of adversity. All leaders must overcome problems in life, even when they can sometimes feel insurmountable. There are solutions to almost any problem, and there are always lessons to be learned from difficult situations.

Personally, once I get over the disappointment and frustration of bad news, deal with the immediate damage, and find level ground, I turn my attention to the lessons I can learn. I am not interested in looking for blame but more so for the improvements or shifts in the business that we can activate to improve ourselves and avoid similar situations in the future. Mistakes happen, but we can almost always overcome them.

The most egregious transgression from leadership is failing to learn lessons and take advantage of the situation to drive systemic improvement in the organization. What did we discover, and what are we going to put in place so this doesn't happen again? This is how we are going to be better.

Leaders can't be afraid of bad news. I certainly don't seek it out, but I would much rather understand the truth and know what I need to fix than remain blissfully unaware. As Tony Robbins says, "Every problem is a gift—without problems we would not grow."

"Never waste a crisis" is one of my favorite sayings and an integral element of how I approach business and life. Though it may sound counterintuitive, the concept is provocative and inspiring. It reminds us that in failure lies opportunity. I'm not suggesting that we find crisis situations pleasing and comfortable, but we can't fear them to the point that they become debilitating and damaging.

How many times has something bad happened to you, or at least what you perceive to be bad, and then you come out better on the other end? I would guess more often than not. I know that the biggest advances that we have made as an ad agency have often been because of a crisis that offered illumination and drove us to make changes.

The phrase "never waste a crisis" means taking advantage of a challenging situation as an opportunity for positive change or growth. That crises often create urgency and expose weaknesses that may have otherwise gone unnoticed during normal circumstances is the basis for the concept. By leveraging the crisis as a catalyst for change, individuals and organizations can emerge from the situation stronger, more resilient, and better equipped to tackle future challenges.

"Never waste a crisis" is a call to action to stay positive and proactive in the face of adversity. It suggests that even the most daunting situations can be opportunities for advancement and growth if approached with the right mindset and perspective.

Often, you don't know there is a problem until something breaks. It is only when things break that we can clearly see what's underneath the surface.

Sometimes you must move the old furniture out of the room to move new furniture in. Isn't that what a crisis does? It moves everything out of the room and leaves you with a clearer view of what you're working with and how you can build back better. How can we possibly renovate our organizations without occasionally moving some things out and rearranging the furniture?

A TINY MOMENT
Turn Setbacks into Springboards

Losing a client in the advertising business is expected. Losing three at roughly the same time, representing 40 percent of net revenue, is not. It's a crisis. Years back, that's what happened to us.

When this was happening, I analyzed the situation and determined that nothing we did pointed to problems with our operation or the work we produced. The reasons for losing the three clients were truly out of our reasonable control: new client ownership, growing in-house departments, and reduced marketing budgets. Sure, we could always improve our work and we were always looking to grow our skills. But the overall quality of our work was strong and not a problem.

The problem we did have was that our marketing and sales were not in a good enough place to absorb this blow. We just didn't have enough activity in the marketplace or prospects in the funnel to convert into new sales. When things are going well, marketing and sales can be an area that suffers from complacency, and we had fallen victim to this. (For another example of how it is always too soon to congratulate yourself, see chapter 8.)

We had a crisis on our hands. If we couldn't recover this revenue, we would have to make layoffs, something we dreaded. My Tiny Moment came when I realized that, yes, we needed to rebuild revenue ASAP, but we also had to learn from this situation so that we would never be caught unprepared again. In that flash, fueled by the jolt of lost revenue, I vowed that I would not waste this "nudge" to get better in the areas where we needed it the most.

How many times have you heard someone say after a bad situation that they came back stronger than ever? That's just what happened to us.

I took a step back and reviewed our entire marketing and sales approach. It was clear that we had been resting on our laurels, relying on word of mouth and repeat business without actively seeking new opportunities. This crisis and the Tiny Moment it sparked was a wake-up call. We needed to be proactive, not reactive.

We assigned someone on staff to focus on the agency as their "client." Under her direction, we revamped our sales strategy, identifying potential prospects and building an outreach plan. I personally got involved in more networking events, conferences, and opportunities to put our agency's name out there. We launched a new marketing campaign, showcasing our recent successes and innovative projects.

It wasn't easy. It took time, effort, and a lot of persistence. There were countless strategy sessions and moments of doubt. But slowly, our hard work started to pay off. We began to see new clients coming in, attracted by our fresh approach and proven track record.

While it took me a while, we were able to rebuild revenue without laying anyone off. In fact, we came out of the crisis stronger and more resilient than ever before. Adversity forced us to confront our weaknesses and address them head-on. We now have a powerful ongoing marketing and sales program for ourselves. Our pipeline is populated, and we have a stream of new prospects and clients.

This experience taught us a valuable lesson: Never waste a crisis. Instead of being paralyzed by fear or despair, we used it as an opportunity to grow and improve, a mindset that has continued to drive our success ever since.

CHAPTER SIXTY-TWO

Deliver Your Best

"DELIVER YOUR best" might be the most obvious sentence written in this book. Obviously, we should deliver our best every day. But what does that really mean, and why should they be words to live by?

It is up to us to consistently strive for alignment with our core values; in other words, we strive to be our best.

Fundamentally, the mantra "Deliver your best" in the leadership sense is a culmination of everything in this book. If we are growing as people and professionals, we will raise the bar for our "best" as we gain experience and seek positive change and growth in ourselves, our capabilities, and our potential. We really want to "be the best we can be" as we strive toward higher and higher standards that we set for ourselves.

To deliver our best means to give our utmost effort, skill, and expertise to accomplish a task or reach a goal. It means utilizing all our abilities and resources to produce the most exceptional outcome possible.

Achieving our best requires setting high standards and continually striving to surpass them through hard work, focus, and determination. It means taking ownership of our work and being accountable for the results.

Core values are the fundamental beliefs and principles that guide our behavior and decision-making. They are the essence of who we are as individuals and organizations and express our most closely held philosophies and guidelines for how we act. In my organizations, we have often proclaimed that our core values "reflect our best behavior delivered on our best days."

However, while core values may inspire us to behave in positive ways, there may be times when we fall short of these values due to various factors such as stress, pressure, or conflicting priorities. Therefore, while core values provide a foundation for our behavior, they do not guarantee that we will always exhibit our best behavior. Various internal and external factors influence our actions, and it is up to us to consistently strive for alignment with our core values; in other words, we strive to be our best.

In his book *The Paradox of Choice*, psychologist Barry Schwartz distinguishes between two types of consumers: satisfiers and maximizers.[1] Satisfiers settle for effort and outcomes that get them by. He is referring to work that is "good enough for government work," a satirical American idiom used to describe something that is merely adequate and meets bare minimum standards.

Maximizers, on the other hand, strive for superiority and greatness. They clearly define the goals they wish to accomplish and then fully commit to them with everything they have. They are "irreplaceable" individuals who not only get the job done but quite often exceed expectations. Compared to satisfiers, maximizers gain more responsibility, get more promotions, and make more money. Most importantly, they get better work done and achieve loftier goals, which results in the rewards they desire in the first place.

Doing your best is synonymous with living out each and every moment to its fullest potential. Granted, we can't be 100 percent on at every moment. Even the most driven among us must take a breath and relax sometimes. But the point is that the overall totality of our effort, our resolve, and our commitment to greatness must be well above the norm to be exceptional people and leaders.

Our pledge to "deliver our best" becomes a reflection of us—our integrity, our steadfastness, and our commitment to excellence. Not only does it represent your self-image, but it also defines how others will draw you in their mind—someone with high standards and a dedication to greatness.

How else would we want to live?

A TINY MOMENT
Good Is Not Good Enough

Steve Jobs was known for his relentless pursuit of excellence. Perhaps no one represented "Good is not good enough" more than he did. At Apple, Jobs constantly pushed his team to transcend the boundaries of "good" to achieve excellence.

For example, Jobs was not satisfied with a merely functional user interface; he wanted it to be intuitive and visually stunning. His demand for excellence led to the creation of a revolutionary user experience. He was also known for his focus on the customer experience. Apple Stores, the Genius Bar, and even the packaging of Apple products were all designed to ensure that customers felt they were getting something special, something more than just a good product.

In the mid-2000s, when Apple was working on the first iPhone, Jobs was presented with the prototype during a design review. The team had worked hard to ensure it met the company's high standards. However, after inspecting the prototype, Jobs wasn't satisfied. He saw potential for more refinement and more innovation. For him, good was simply not good enough.

One reaction that highlights this attitude was Jobs's feedback on the iPhone screen. Initially, the prototype had a plastic screen, which was the industry norm at the time. Jobs knew that plastic scratched too easily, compromising the user experience and the product's longevity. He insisted on using glass instead. The team argued it would be too difficult and expensive, but Jobs was adamant. In a Tiny Moment that reinforced Jobs's "deliver your best" philosophy to those around him and everyone at Apple, he famously told them, "This is what we're going to do. Make it work."

His edict pushed the team to explore new technologies and work with suppliers to create a special kind of glass, which eventually became Gorilla Glass. This innovation not only met Jobs's high standards but also set a new industry benchmark for durability and quality.

Through these actions, Jobs helped his team understand that in a competitive and fast-evolving industry, good was not good enough. He instilled in them the belief that excellence should be the standard. This philosophy not only drove the success of the iPhone but also cemented Apple's reputation for innovation and quality.

Jobs's leadership demonstrated that by pushing beyond good, you could achieve greatness. This story of the iPhone's development is a testament to how his insistence on excellence helped Apple create products that not only met but exceeded customer expectations, leading to monumental success.

Final Thought

FEEL SOME level of responsibility in assembling some of the tools that have shaped my life and leadership style and passing them on to you. My hope is that this book will assist you in crafting your own legacy, empowering you to choose how to utilize these tools to become the best version of yourself. My legacy is in part reflected in you and the choices you make.

We often contemplate the impact we have on others and the mark we leave behind. How have our actions contributed positively to the lives of those around us? How do our actions leave a positive imprint on those around us? What legacy are we striving to construct? Arnold Schwarzenegger's poignant words, "My legacy is you," resonate deeply with me, capturing the essence of immortality through the lives we influence.

Compiling this collection of tools and Tiny Moments is a gesture rooted in the belief that our legacies are interwoven with the knowledge we share. Hopefully, this book becomes a vessel of empowerment, guiding you on the path toward your own unique legacy and granting you the autonomy to utilize these tools to inspire a masterpiece version of yourself.

In your journey, remember that your time will be marked by the choices you make, the impact you have, and the person you have become. As you embark on this transformative process, my sincere hope is that these pages not only serve as a guide that you can go back to now and again but also inspire profound introspection, pushing you to delve deeper into the meaningfulness of your existence. Your journey is not just yours—it's a continuation of the legacies before you, your own legacy in the making, and other legacies yet to come.

Make me proud.

Acknowledgments

TO MY wife, Carole, and my three kids, Matt, Kara, and Alex—For teaching me that true mentorship starts at home. It's there, in the daily moments, where we teach each other the most valuable lessons: love, balance, and patience. You have been my greatest teachers and my unwavering foundation.

To my mother—For being an extraordinary role model for my brothers and me as we learned our way through life. You taught us how to be kind and strong and led by example in every way that mattered. The values you instilled in me have been my guidepost both personally and professionally.

To my brother, Bill—For your support and encouragement throughout the years. You have been a consistent presence in my life, always demonstrating the power of positivity and resilience. More importantly, you helped me internalize and put into practice all of what our mother taught us, making those lessons a core part of who we are today.

To Shadley Grei—This book simply wouldn't have happened without you. From the earliest stages, when it was just a flicker of an idea, you believed in its potential. You were my first inspiration, ongoing cheerleader, and indispensable advisor, always reminding me that my message was worth sharing and that this book could be something worth reading.

To Keith Kryzak—Your exceptional design expertise and keen eye for detail brought this book to life with clarity and style.

To Tami Brouillette—For your thoughtful, precise, and always exceptional editorial guidance. Your care and insight helped elevate this work to be its best.

To all the incredible teams I've worked with throughout my career—You've been my teachers, collaborators, and motivators. A special thank you to the team at EVR Advertising, where I spent the final chapter of my official career. You were my laboratory for growth, helping me put years of learning into practice, refine what leadership looks like in action, and pursue my lifelong goal of always improving as a leader.

To my buddies Dan Wessels and Steve McKenna—For your genuine interest, encouragement, and belief in this project all along the way. Your support and friendship helped keep me going.

And to Dee Kerr, Brian Welch, Tess Newton, and the entire team at Greenleaf Book Group Publishing—Your professionalism, creativity, and partnership made this process a true pleasure. Thank you for guiding this book into the world with care.

Each of you has been part of this journey in a unique and meaningful way. This book, and the lessons it imparts, is a reflection of you and all the people who have shaped me throughout my life.

Notes

INTRODUCTION

1. Harlan Cleveland, *The Knowledge Executive: Leadership in an Information Society* (Truman Talley Books, 1985), 160.

THE BIG THREE

1. Grace Hopper, quoted in Esther Surden, "Privacy Laws May Usher in 'Defensive DP': Hooper," *Computerworld* 10, no. 4 (January 26, 1976).

2. Henry Ford, quoted in *Henry Ford's Own Story: How a Farmer Boy Rose to the Power That Goes With Many Millions Yet Never Lost Touch With Humanity* by Rose Wilder Lane (Garden City Publishing, 1917), 99.

3. Thomas A. Edison, quoted in *Edison: His Life and Inventions* by Frank Lewis Dyer and Thomas Commerford Martin (Harper & Brothers, 1910), 463.

4. Patrick Lencioni, *The Five Dysfunctions of a Team: A Leadership Fable* (Jossey-Bass, 2002), 43.

5. Brian Tracy, "The glue that holds all relationships together— including the relationship between the leader and the led is trust," Facebook, March 25, 2014, https://www.facebook.com/BrianTracyPage/photos/ the-glue-that-holds-all-relationships-together-including-the-relationship- betwee/10152074283378460/?_rdr.

6. Paul J. Zak, "The Neuroscience of Trust," *Harvard Business Review*, January–February 2017, 84–90.

7. John Quincy Adams, quoted in William A. Cohen, *Leadership in the Twenty-First Century* (McGraw-Hill, 1990), 22.

8. Terri Trespicio, "Stop Searching for Your Passion | Terri Trespicio | TEDxKC," YouTube, TEDx Talk, September 14, 2015, https://www.youtube.com/ watch?v=6MBaFL7sCb8.

9. Simon Sinek, "How Do You Find Your Passion?," Facebook, video, August 13, 2019, https://www.facebook.com/simonsinek/videos/how-do-you-find-your-passion/2810926835588935/.

10. Erika Andersen, *Leading So People Will Follow* (Wiley, 2012), 62.

1. LEADERSHIP IS ACTION, NOT A TITLE
1. Chen Zhang et al., "Why Capable People Are Reluctant to Lead," *Harvard Business Review,* December 17, 2020, https://hbr.org/2020/12/why-capable-people-are-reluctant-to-lead.

2. ARE LEADERS BORN OR MADE?
1. Richard D. Arvey et al., "The Determinants of Leadership Role Occupancy: Genetic and Personality Factors," *The Leadership Quarterly* 17, no. 1 (February 2006): 1–20, https://doi.org/10.1016/j.leaqua.2005.10.009.

3. BE THE FIRST TO STRIVE
1. Neil Patel, "Your Secret Mental Weapon: 'Don't Let the Perfect Be the Enemy of the Good,'" *Entrepreneur*, August 31, 2015, https://www.entrepreneur.com/living/your-secret-mental-weapon-dont-let-the-perfect-be-the/249676.

5. WHEN DID YOU FIND YOUR VOICE?
1. Stephen R. Covey, *The 8th Habit: From Effectiveness to Greatness* (Free Press, 2004), 5.

2. James M. Kouzes and Barry Z. Posner, *The Leadership Challenge: How to Make Extraordinary Things Happen in Organizations* (Jossey-Bass, 2012), 45.

6. OWN YOUR LEADERSHIP BRAND
1. Sally Percy, "Six Ways to Build Your Leadership Brand," *Forbes*, October 7, 2022, https://www.forbes.com/sites/sallypercy/2022/10/07/six-ways-to-build-your-personal-brand/.

2. Tom Peters, "What a 'Personal Brand' Is NOT," *tompeters!* (blog), January 16, 2009, https://tompeters.com/2009/01/what-a-personal-brand-is-not/.

7. HAVE HUMILITY
1. Plato, *The Republic*, trans. Benjamin Jowett (Dover Publications, 2000), 304.

2. Donald H. Rumsfeld, "Rumsfeld's Rules," *The Wall Street Journal*, January 29, 2001, https://www.wsj.com/articles/SB980725598174002005.

8. IT'S ALWAYS TOO SOON TO CONGRATULATE YOURSELF

1. Merriam-Webster, s.v. "complacency," accessed October 28, 2024, https://www.merriam-webster.com/dictionary/complacency.

2. Edwin Catmull in Jonah Sachs, "Pixar's Ed Catmull on How Collaborative Competition Drives Success," *Fast Company*, February 24, 2017, https://www.fastcompany.com/3068491/ pixars-ed-catmull-on-how-collaborative-competition-drives-success.

3. Warren Bennis, *On Becoming a Leader* (Basic Books, 2009), 42.

10. BE BRAVELY TRANSPARENT

1. Jack Welch, *Winning* (HarperCollins, 2005), 27.

2. "Trust, Tools and Teamwork: What Workers Want," Slack, October 3, 2018, https://slack.com/blog/transformation/ trust-tools-and-teamwork-what-workers-want.

11. CREDIBILITY IS EARNED

1. James M. Kouzes and Barry Z. Posner, *The Leadership Challenge: How to Make Extraordinary Things Happen in Organizations* (Jossey-Bass, 2012).

2. Kouzes and Posner, *The Leadership Challenge*.

12. EAT THE FROG

1. Mark Twain, quoted in Brian Tracy, *Eat That Frog!: 21 Great Ways to Stop Procrastinating and Get More Done in Less Time* (Berrett-Koehler Publishers, 2001), 1.

2. Charles Bankston, "7 Steps For Building a Transparent and Trustworthy Company Culture," *Forbes*, February 28, 2020.

14. BE CLEAR ABOUT THE WHY

1. David Benjamin and David Komlos, "Has Your Organization Stopped Asking Questions?," *Forbes*, September 26, 2022, https://www.forbes.com/sites/ benjaminkomlos/2022/09/26/has-your-organization-stopped-asking-questions/.

2. Simon Sinek, *Start with Why: How Great Leaders Inspire Everyone to Take Action* (2009), 151.

3. Jacinta Jimenez, *The Burnout Fix: Overcome Overwhelm, Beat Busy, and Sustain Success in the New World of Work* (McGraw-Hill Education, 2021), 52.

16. CREATE URGENCY

1. John P. Kotter, *A Sense of Urgency* (Harvard Business Press, 2008), 6–8.

17. THE WORST DECISION IS NO DECISION

1. "Theodore Roosevelt Quotes," Theodore Roosevelt Center, accessed November 26, 2024, https://www.theodorerooseveltcenter.org/Learn-About-TR/TR-Quotes/.

19. BE A ROLE MODEL OF CHARACTER AND ETHICS

1. Kenneth H. Blanchard and Margret McBride, *The One Minute Apology: A Powerful Way to Make Things Better* (William Marrow, 2003), 33.

20. TRUE CHARACTER IS REVEALED IN ADVERSITY

1. Warren Buffett, Berkshire Hathaway Shareholder Letter, Berkshire Hathaway, Inc., February 28, 2002, https://www.berkshirehathaway.com/2001ar/2001letter.html.

21. BE MINDFUL OF YOUR POWER

1. Jonah Lehrer, "How Power Corrupts," *WIRED*, May 18, 2011, https://www.wired.com/2011/05/how-power-corrupts/.

2. Ian Robertson, *The Winner Effect: How Power Affects Your Brain* (Bloomsbury, 2012), 57.

3. Dacher Keltner, *The Power Paradox: How We Gain and Lose Influence* (Penguin Press, 2016).

24. BIRDS OF A FEATHER FLOCK TOGETHER

1. Tony Robbins and Jospeh McClendon III, *Unlimited Power: A Black Choice* (Simon & Schuster, 1997), 397.

2. Jack Welch, *Jack: What I've Learned Leading a Great Company and Great People* (Headline, 2002).

25. WIN HEARTS TO WIN MINDS

1. John Burroughs, *The Art of Seeing Things: Essays* (Syracuse University Press, 2001): 59.

26. BE VULNERABLE

1. Patrick Lencioni, *The Five Dysfunctions of a Team: A Leadership Fable* (Jossey-Bass, 2002).

2. Simon Sinek, "To be authentic is to be imperfect," Facebook, June 28, 2018, https://www.facebook.com/simonsinek/posts/to-be-authentic-is-to-be-imperfectauthenticity-is-about-imperfection-and-authent/10156483042771499/.

27. REMEMBER NAMES

1. Dale Carnegie, *How to Win Friends and Influence People* (Simon & Schuster, 1936), 113.

29. DELEGATE OR BUST

1. Jesse Sostrin, "To Be a Great Leader, You Have to Learn How to Delegate Well," *Harvard Business Review*, July 25, 2017, https://hbr.org/2017/10/to-be-a-great-leader-you-have-to-learn-how-to-delegate-well.

31. BE GRAY

1. Steven B. Sample, *The Contrarian's Guide to Leadership* (Jossey-Bass, 2002), 7–8.

32. WHO'S GOT THE MONKEY?

1. William Oncken Jr. and Donald L. Wass, "Management Time: Who's Got the Monkey?" *Harvard Business Review*, November–December 1974.

2. Stephen R. Covey, "Making Time for Gorillas," in William Oncken Jr. and Donald L. Wass, "Management Time: Who's Got the Monkey?" *Harvard Business Review*, November–December 1999, https://hbr.org/1999/11/management-time-whos-got-the-monkey.

33. STAY BALANCED BETWEEN BEING AND DOING

1. Michael Carroll, "Meet the Author Michael Carroll," Awake at Work with Michael Carroll, accessed November 14, 2024, https://www.awakeatwork.net/content/meet-author-michael-carroll.

2. Pam Hernandez, "Leadership Focus on 'Being' versus 'Doing," *The Right Reflection* (blog), June 15, 2022, https://therightreflection.com/positive-psychology/leadership-focus-on-being-versus-doing/.

35. BE A LIFELONG LEARNER

1. Gemma Leigh Roberts, "Weekly Mindset Matters Newsletter," Mindset Matters, July 12, 2023.

36. MANAGE BY WALKING AROUND

1. Tom Peters, "Excellence: MBWA," YouTube, August 25, 2010, https://www.youtube.com/watch?v=X01ZWvtX_ZM.

2. Texas Bix Bender, *Don't Squat with Your Spurs On: A Cowboy's Guide to Life* (Gibbs Smith, 1997).

3. Wharton School of the University of Pennsylvania, "MBWA: Translating Management By Walking Around to a Remote World," Knowledge@Wharton, March 15, 2021.

37. TRUST BUT VERIFY

1. Claus Langfred, "Too Much of a Good Thing? Negative Effects of High Trust and Individual Autonomy in Self-Managing Teams," *Academy of Management Journal* 47, no. 3 (2004): 385–99, https://doi.org/10.2307/20159588.

38. ENFORCE ACCOUNTABILITY

1. Stephen R. Covey, *The 7 Habits of Highly Effective People: Powerful Lessons in Personal Change* (Free Press, 1989), 71.

2. Karim Bashay, "The Importance of Accountability," *HR magazine*, August, 21, 2017, https://www.hrmagazine.co.uk/content/features/the-importance-of-accountability/.

39. PERSONIFY THE HEART OF A SERVANT

1. Robert K. Greenleaf, *The Servant as Leader* (Center for Applied Studies, 1970).

2. Itay Talgam, "Lead Like the Great Conductors," TED Talk, February 2009, https://www.ted.com/talks/itay_talgam_lead_like_the_great_conductors.

43. FAILING FORWARD

1. Thomas H. Palmer, *The Teacher's Manual: Being an Exposition of an Efficient and Economical System of Education, Suited to the Wants of a Free People* (Marsh, Capen, Lyon, and Webb, 1840), 223.

44. RECOGNIZE AND CELEBRATE

1. Emily Lorenz, "How to Bridge the Generational Gap in Recognition," Gallup Workplace, August 29, 2022, https://www.gallup.com/workplace/396470/bridge-generational-gap-recognition.aspx.

2. Sheila McClear, "Millennial and Gen Z Workers Have Low Job Satisfaction and Really Want Rewards and Prizes," Ladders, September 4, 2019, https://www.theladders.com/career-advice/millennial-and-gen-z-workers-have-low-job-satisfaction-and-really-want-rewards-and-prizes.

3. Amanda Cross, "26 Employee Recognition Statistics You Need to Know in 2024," *Nectar Blog*, last updated October 30, 2024, https://nectarhr.com/blog/employee-recognition-statistics

4. Gallup and Workhuman, "Amplifying Wellbeing at Work and Beyond through the Power of Recognition," Gallup, May 2022, https://assets.ctfassets.net/hff6luki1ys4/Qu9UUxsvV9iJyouN23M6t/acf085b6de297317538bd43de686d023/amplifying-wellbeing-at-work-and-beyond-through-recognition.pdf.

45. PRAISE IN PUBLIC, CRITICIZE IN PRIVATE

1. Winston Churchill, quoted in Kingsley Martin, "Winston Churchill Interviewed in 1939: 'The British People Would Rather Go Down Fighting,'" *New Statesman*, January 6, 2014, https://www.newstatesman.com/uncategorized/2014/01/british-people-would-rather-go-down-fighting.

2. Joshua Harris, *I Kissed Dating Goodbye* (Multnomah Books, 1997), 89.

48. TAKE FUN SERIOUSLY

1. Naomi Bagdonas and Connor Diemand-Yauman, "Laugh More, Lead Better," McKinsey & Company, April 15, 2021, https://www.mckinsey.com/featured-insights/leadership/laugh-more-lead-better.

2. Barbara Plester and Ann Hutchinson, "Fun Times: The Relationship Between Fun and Workplace Engagement," *Employee Relations* 38, no. 3 (2016): 332–350, https://doi.org/10.1108/ER-03-2014-0027.

49. FEEDBACK IS A GIFT

1. Ken Blanchard, *The One Minute Manager* (William Morrow, 1982), 68.

50. EXPECT GROWTH

1. Amy Adkins and Brandon Rigoni, "Millennials Want Jobs to Be Development Opportunities," Gallup Workplace, June 30, 2016, https://www.gallup.com/workplace/236438/millennials-jobs-development-opportunities.aspx.

51. BE INTERESTED, NOT INTERESTING

1. Dale Carnegie, *How to Win Friends and Influence People* (Simon & Schuster, 1936), 92.

2. Celeste Headlee, "10 Ways to Have a Better Conversation," TED Talk, March 2015, https://www.ted.com/talks/celeste_headlee_10_ways_to_have_a_better_conversation.

3. Headlee, "10 Ways to Have a Better Conversation."

4. Stephen R. Covey, *The 7 Habits of Highly Effective People: Powerful Lessons in Personal Change* (Free Press, 1989), 71.

52. DELIVER PLUS ONE

1. Ken Blanchard and Sheldon Bowles, *Raving Fans: A Revolutionary Approach to Customer Service* (William Morrow, 1993), 45.

53. WORST IDEA GOES FIRST

1. Google, "Understand Team Effectiveness," Google re:Work, accessed November 22, 2024, https://rework.withgoogle.com/en/guides/understanding-team-effectiveness#measure-team-effectiveness.

54. ENCOURAGE "INTRAPRENEURSHIP"

1. Ute Stephan, Mark Hart, and Cord-Christian Drews, "Understanding Motivations for Entrepreneurship: A Review of Recent Research Evidence," Enterprise Research Centre, February 2015, https://www.enterpriseresearch.ac.uk/wp-content/uploads/2015/02/Understanding-Motivations-for-Entrepreneur-ship-White-Paper-No-10.pdf.

55. YOU'RE ON STAGE. ALWAYS.

1. Paul Boyles, "Leaders Are Always on Stage," LinkedIn post, May 6, 2023, https://www.linkedin.com/pulse/leaders-always-stage-paul-boyles-sphr-shrm-scp/.

2. Peter Drucker, *The Effective Executive: The Definitive Guide to Getting the Right Things Done* (HarperCollins, 1967), 113.

56. TAKE THE BULLET

1. Elizabeth B. Lozano and Sean M. Laurent, "The Effects of Admitting Fault versus Shifting Blame on Expectations for Others to Do the Same," *PLos ONE* 14, no. 3 (March 7, 2019), https://doi.org/10.1371/journal.pone.0213276.

2. Arnold H. Glasgow, quoted in *Inspiration for Leaders: A Collection of Wisdom*, ed. Richard H. Johnson (Springer, 1992), 74.

57. SACRIFICE RAISES THE LEVEL OF COMMITMENT

1. *Office Space*, directed by Mike Judge (Los Angeles: 20th Century Fox, 1999).

2. John C. Maxwell, *The 21 Irrefutable Laws of Leadership: Follow Them and People Will Follow You* (Thomas Nelson, 1998), 142.

3. Ralph Waldo Emerson, *Essays, First Series 1841*, "Compensation," American Transcendentalism, accessed November 25, 2024, https://archive.vcu.edu/english/engweb/transcendentalism/authors/emerson/essays/compensation.html.

58. WELCOME THE MESSENGER OF CONFLICT

1. Frank Sonnenberg, "Do You Live in the Dark? The Danger of Being Uninformed," Frank Sonnenberg Online, (blog), October 16, 2018, https://www.franksonnenbergonline.com/blog/do-you-live-in-the-dark-the-danger-of-being-uninformed/.

59. NO DATA WITHOUT STORY, NO STORY WITHOUT DATA

1. Brené Brown, "The Power of Vulnerability," TEDTalk, June, 2010, https://www.ted.com/talks/brene_brown_the_power_of_vulnerability/transcript?subtitle=en.

62. DELIVER YOUR BEST

1. Barry Schwartz, *The Paradox of Choice: Why More Is Less* (Harper Perennial, 2004), 17.

About the Author

JEFF EISENBERG is a seasoned executive with over four decades of experience spanning business and sports management. As owner and president of EVR Advertising from 2009 to 2024, Jeff transformed the agency into a full-service marketing powerhouse known for its strategic insights and impactful campaigns. Under his visionary leadership, EVR became a trusted partner for health care, senior living, and a diverse array of New England–based clients, delivering specialized services in market research, branding, creative design, media planning, and digital solutions. His commitment to cultivating a high-performance team, fostering personal growth, and championing collaborative innovation led EVR to exponential revenue growth, solidifying its reputation for excellence in an ever-evolving marketing landscape.

Before his time at EVR, Jeff's leadership journey was marked by notable achievements in the professional sports industry. He spent the first two decades of his career in pivotal senior roles with the Philadelphia Phillies, Milwaukee Brewers, Buffalo Sabres, and Portland Pirates, laying the foundation for his expertise in organizational growth and brand building.

In 2000, the Los Angeles Kings appointed Jeff as the inaugural president of the Manchester Monarchs Hockey Club, a new American Hockey League franchise. As the Monarchs' first employee, he built the organization from the ground up, establishing a vibrant and enduring brand within the community. His vision, strategic acumen, and commitment to fan engagement propelled the Monarchs to the top of the league in attendance, winning numerous accolades and firmly embedding the team as an iconic New Hampshire brand. For his contributions, Jeff was awarded the AHL's Executive of the Year in 2004, recognizing his role in transforming the Monarchs into one of the league's most successful franchises.

An active community leader, Jeff has dedicated significant time to various boards and committees, including the Catholic Medical Center, Greater Manchester Chamber of Commerce, Boy Scouts of America's Daniel Webster Council, Saint Anselm College Center for Ethics in Society, and the Mental Health Center of Greater Manchester. His community involvement underscores his commitment to service and the positive impact of local leadership.

Jeff holds a BS degree in Economics from Vanderbilt University and an MS degree in Sport Management from the University of Massachusetts. Beyond his professional achievements, Jeff has shared his expertise with emerging business leaders, serving as an adjunct professor of Sport Management, previously at Southern New Hampshire University and currently at the Franklin Pierce University Business School.

Jeff's career—from sports management to advertising—demonstrates a dedication to building organizations, inspiring teams, and fostering community connections. Whether shaping fan-favorite sports franchises or creating impactful marketing campaigns, Jeff exemplifies a legacy rooted in strategic vision, a passion for people-focused leadership, and a relentless commitment to organizational excellence.